Horizons The Cookbook

Rich Landau & Kate Jacoby

Book Publishing Company
Summertown, Tennessee

Questions regarding cookbook recipes or cooking methods can be sent directly to galaxychef@aol.com. We also invite you to visit the restaurant website at www.horizonscafe.com .

Inka Chips is a trademark of Inka Crops North America.
Michel-Schlumber Cabernet is a product of Michel-Schlumberger Wines.
Native Forest is a trademark of Edwards & Sons Trading Company, Inc.
Vegenaise is a registered trademark of Follow Your Heart's Natural Foods Market and Cafe.
Your Morning on CN8 is a production of The Comcast Network.

Printed in Canada.

Book Publishing Company
415 Farm Road
PO Box 99
Summertown, TN 38483
888-260-8458
www.bookpubco.com

Landau, Rich, 1967-
 Horizons: the cookbook : gourmet meatless cuisine / Rich Landau & Kate Jacoby.
   p. cm.
 Includes index.
 ISBN 1-57067-179-6
 1. Vegetarian cookery. I. Jacoby, Kate, 1980- II. Horizons Cafe (Willow Grove, Pa.) III. Title.

TX837
641.5'636—dc22   2004027588

Photography and book design by Donna Gentile Wierzbowski of DG Design & Photography

*In memory of
our grandmothers:
Eleanor Witz and
Mary Ketchell*

Table of Contents

Foreword

. . . .

Only the uninitiated would think that vegetarian food is a one-way trip to Blandsville. One visit to Willow Grove's Horizons Café should dispel any such misconception.

Beyond the open kitchen, the walls are ablaze with earthy, vibrant colors. Paintings of cacti, howling wolves, palm trees, seascapes and guitars—some reminiscent of Picasso or Frida Kahlo—bring a smile to your face.

At Horizons the sun is everywhere—on the walls; on the open faces of chef/owner Rich Landau as he prepares a seitan special or Kate Jacoby as she fashions a vegan dessert; on the surprised faces of guests, as they smell, then see, then taste the incredible concoctions placed on their tables. The musical soundtrack often sounds Latino, and many dishes have sun-splashed origins. This is South of the Border...with a more than a scintilla of sophistication.

In Horizons, Rich and Kate have brought a slice of the city to the suburbs. Their restaurant is a pretty funky affair that melds a little Mexican and Mediterranean with touches of all the world's great cuisines. And this remarkable young couple enjoy sharing, with any guests who ask, their own thoughts on vegetarianism—from their belief that you don't have to eat animal products to have a satisfying meal, to their joy in creating wonderful culinary magic that entices the hesitant or skeptical to take that first step into a brave new dining experience.

I've been writing my Ticket to Dining column for nearly a dozen years, so nothing much on the dining scene comes as a great surprise. But I must admit that, like so many "outsiders" to vegetarian cooking, I was not prepared for the harvest of new horizons that Rich and Kate introduced to my palate.

But the appetizers and entrees are vegetarian, Rich! And all the desserts, Kate, are vegan. What makes them look, smell, and taste so good?

Horizons: The Cookbook attempts to answer that question and, in the process, opens up sun-splashed windows into one of the world's least heralded approaches to dining. Horizons' menu is remarkably adventuresome and can be surprisingly easy to conjure up.

Rich and Kate have translated their passion about food and cooking into one of the most exciting menus anywhere in Montgomery County. This cookbook brings that menu, and the inspiration behind it, into your very own kitchen.

FRANK D. QUATTRONE
Ticket Editor
Montgomery Newspapers

Acknowledgments

. . . .

We would like to extend a heartfelt thank-you to everyone who has made it possible for us to love what we do. Looking out at the dining room on a busy Saturday night and knowing that all these people have come out to eat a vegetarian meal on a very precious weekend night is the most incredible gratification. Our work is our passion, and we are forever indebted to those who enable us to continue to do something that we love. This book is a tribute to the thousands of people who have walked through the many doors of Horizons over the years and especially to those who have asked the now infamous question, "When is the cookbook coming out?" Well, now we have an answer! We really hope you enjoy it.

We would also like to give more specific thanks to: Jeff & Ross for helping to try out recipes and for giving valuable input; Bill for tons of technology assistance, input, and holding reflectors for long periods of time; Sue & Jose for artistic inspiration and encouragement; Frank Quattrone for his advice from the world of editing and publishing; Dotsy, Mike, Rue, Sue & Rob (Rich's family) for their unending support...

And most of all, Donna, for her incredible sense of humor, her work ethic, her creativity, and her enthusiasm. Thanks to Donna, the book is finally here.

The Origin

· ·

As I sit in this TACA flight bound for Honduras, I am working on the final text for this project that has been a long time in the making—Horizons: The Cookbook.

Horizons has been a reality for almost 10 years now. I have watched it grow, and it has watched me grow. Now is the time for this project to finally come to fruition. So what has brought you and me to these pages together right now? Well, it seems the concept of Horizons found me before I found it.

I grew up in a typical Philadelphia suburban household. Fish sticks, baked chicken, turkey tetrazzini, meatloaf, and the likes could have been found on my family's dinner table on any given weeknight. I had a food-loving family; eating was an event, a celebration, a feast. My mom and I loved to create in the kitchen, spicing things up and "doctoring up" recipes from my required Home-Ec class. Our kitchen was always alive with flavors, spice, adventure, and creative culinary explorations. I loved food and never really worried about it too much. When I was very young, my inquisitive mind was in overdrive one night after an indulgence in a cup of hot chocolate. I asked my dad, "Where does steak come from?" "From cows," he replied. So I pictured a cow laying a steak like a chicken would lay an egg. No problem...and the Landau feasts continued with no protest.

As I got older I learned the truth. The cows were being slaughtered and we were eating "THEM." I was horrified, but I faced a unique dilemma. By now I had grown to absolutely love the taste of animal meat, but I was also in love with animals.

My ethical aversion to animal meat is what moved me to try to change my diet. But how does a "meat-and-potatoes" kid change his diet so drastically? Keep in mind, this was the late 70's; there were no veggie burgers, sausages, or pepperoni, which are so readily available today. It was wheat germ, granola, and alfalfa sprouts—fine for my rabbit friends, but no way was I going to eat this stuff!

I struggled for years, going back and forth through chicken and fish stages and cheese hoagies, until it was time to put my passion for cooking to the test and create a cuisine that would satisfy me and not make me miss the meat.

To start off, what is "meatless cuisine"? I have been asked to define it many a time. The questions usually come phrased as: "You're vegetarian, what do you eat?" I think "vegetarian food" is too often confused and used interchangeably with "health food." Yes, vegetarian food is naturally healthy, provided you do not exist on a diet of eggplant parmigiana and fried mozzarella.

Health is an important aspect of Horizons food. I want our guests to leave feeling great and believing they can eat there anytime. But when the words "health food" come into play, I think you can scare off a whole bunch of people that would otherwise embrace such an adventurous dining experience. The word "vegetarian" has been associated with health food markets for too long. So to begin with, I prefer the term "meatless cuisine."

To me, any dish on this great planet can be made meatless, which is where the Horizons philosophy starts. Find the great dishes of the world, clean them up, and take out the meat. Then you have meatless cuisine.

It can be steak and potatoes, paella, bouillabaisse, cioppino, gumbo…
anything you want. This book will show you how to make your own
global cuisine without meat.

I strive to create dishes with intriguing flavors, complimentary
textures, an exotic ingredient or two, and, most of all, depth. Not only
must the dish taste good to the palate, it must go right into one's spirit
and soul. Nothing on the plate should offend—all ingredients must
work together to create a gastronomic harmony.

So what inspires me? I love the tropics with its water and beautiful
mountain scenery, but it is the coast that moves me the most. Whether it
is an island with 360 degrees of the stuff, or the southern coastline of
almost anywhere. It is where the land meets the sea and the sea meets
the sky that I feel most at home and connected to our natural world. As I
write this, we are flying over Cuba, and I dream of the wonderful aromas
coming from tiny kitchens and outdoor cafés: frijoles, plantains, calabazas,
arroz, lime, and garlic. The tropics are a food lover's fantasy. There's
nothing fancy or ostentatious about tropical food. It is simple and fresh
and makes a very short journey from field to plate, and I love it for that.

Up here in the northeast, our restaurants love to embrace and
embellish such cultural simplicities, adorning everything we do with
fried leek cages, colorful oils, and intricate stacking presentations—
not to mention plates that could be put in an art gallery! It's my day
job, and I love it more all the time. But how nice it is to come down
to where human and earth are not separated by so much "stuff"
that we can enjoy the plain old things the good earth gives us with
so little tampering.

Another coastal area that has always captured my culinary dreams
is the European Riviera: Greece, Italy, France, and Spain. My travels there
have not been as extensive, but the tastes I have had leave me yearning
for the Mediterranean coasts—the olives, lemons, tomatoes, fresh

parsley, and basil as well as the beautiful breads and, best of all, extra virgin olive oil, one of the greatest food products in the world.

You will find many "coast-inspired" recipes in this cookbook. Some are versions of dishes I have experienced in my travels, while some are ideas I thought of while floating in the azure waters of the tropics. Some are actual Horizons menu dishes, and some just happen to come to me out of the blue.

I understand how busy people are these days and that you don't have a professional kitchen at your disposal. I am humbly reminded of how different it is to cook at home when I do so on my "weekends." Within these pages, I have tried to provide as many options, shortcuts, tips, hints, and substitutions as possible so that these recipes will actually be a source of enjoyment for you and not just work.

Always remember to be aware of what you are doing when you are cooking. Don't just follow a recipe—cook it…create it! Let the techniques become a part of you. Also, learn to feel out the properties of your ingredients and how they may vary. Fresh produce changes constantly. The juice of a lime today may give you three times more than the lime you will juice next week. The ginger you used last recipe might have been sweet, but the piece you have now is spicy. Onions can be hot or sweet. Herbs can be bitter when old. Peppers can vary enormously.

The point is to learn to adjust—learn to taste and to add balance. If you just follow a recipe, like a science project, you will have more of an "end result" rather than a creation, which is why it is important to be a part of what you are doing. Cooking is not just nourishment; it is a life source, a passion, and an adventure for the senses. Enjoy it.

RSL
Somewhere over the Western Caribbean
26 May 2002

Getting Started

. . . .

For those of you who are new to meatless cooking, we recommend that you read this section in its entirety to get acquainted with the cooking techniques, terminology, and recommended spices. For those of you who have been vegetarian for a while, perhaps you can find a new or interesting way to prepare your favorite food or hints for cooking a particular item that has given you past trouble. You will also find secrets, tips, and special touches that we use at the restaurant.

We've separated this cookbook into seven main sections and an index. Use the Getting Started *section as your springboard to creative cooking. Taking a few minutes now to review the information will help you get things underway quickly. We've included over 100 recipes within these pages, from a beginning appetizer, such as Seitan Skewers with Curry BBQ Sauce to a sweet ending, like the Mexican Chocolate Tower, and every dish and condiment in between.*

If fat intake is a concern to you, we've included recipe variations to reduce fat grams as well as calories. Look for the CTF *(Cut-the-Fat) symbol within the recipe's ingredients list.*

Lastly, have fun and never be afraid to adjust. No recipe ever comes out exactly the same way twice, so enjoy yourself!

Working with Tofu

. . . .

Tofu has, unfortunately, become the evil icon of vegetarianism. It seems tofu is responsible for turning so many people off and giving the whole vegetarian thing a bad rep. It's been my life's work to make tofu palatable. I have to say, I love the stuff, but it took me years to learn how to prepare it properly.

So what is tofu? Tofu is a soy-bean-curd cake. Very simply, soybeans are boiled, a coagulating agent called *nigari* is added, and a curd comes to the surface, almost like a cheese. It's then skimmed off and pressed into bricks. Kate and I had the pleasure of visiting a tofu kitchen once in Allentown. We drove up expecting to smell the incense, part the beads, and see a few hippies laboring away listening to the "Dead." What we found instead was an ultra modern, Willy Wonka-esque machine-world fantasy land. It really impressed us how far this has all come.

So, how did I find tofu? Well maybe like the rest of you, I first tried it in a bad Chinese restaurant and spit it right out. It reminded me of when I would chew my eraser in second grade. Subsequently, I shunned it for years.

As my culinary explorations continued and I gained more confidence, I tried embracing tofu for what it is. Rather than follow the already navigated paths of throwing small pieces of tofu into a big stir fry to try to "absorb" the rest of the flavors around it, I decided to focus on the tofu. Low and behold, tofu actually can taste good! Fresh, quality tofu cooked through the center, with a golden crust, has convinced many of our customers that tofu is a pleasure for vegetarians and meat eaters alike.

My favorite two ways to prepare tofu are to pan-sear it with a spice crust or to grill it after marinating it for hours. We will go into detail for both of these methods on the next two pages, as well as several alternative preparations that we also use at the restaurant. Keep in mind that tofu will keep for more than a week if you always keep it completely covered in water and change the water at least every other day. When you are ready to use it, leave it out on the counter to let some of the water drain out. You also can press it under a book or frying pan to make it denser if you like, but that little bit of extra water remaining inside can make tofu nice and juicy. It's up to you.

Pan-Searing Tofu

This is the restaurant's signature way of cooking tofu. With minimal oil, the result—once mastered—is a wonderful golden crust that is full of flavor. The keys are salt and pepper here. Use whole spices, grind them separately in your coffee mill until they are coarse, and then mix them together. Use whatever supporting spices you like or those that you have available. Here is a basic recipe to get you started.

Tofu Spice

2 tablespoon coarse salt
2 tablespoon peppercorns, black or mixed
1 teaspoon coriander seeds
1 teaspoon caraway seeds
1 teaspoon fennel seeds
1 teaspoon cumin seeds
1 teaspoon celery seeds (do not grind)

Procedure

1. Liberally coat a 1-inch slice of tofu with the tofu spice on one side.
2. Place a shallow layer of canola or olive oil in a sauté pan.
3. Heat until very hot (you'll see slight ripples, but don't let it smoke).
4. Turn off the heat and gently lay in the tofu, spice side down.
5. Return to heat, spice other side, and cook until bottom looks golden.
6. Turn off the heat and <u>carefully</u> flip it with tongs or a spatula.
7. Turn the heat back on and cook the other side until golden brown.
Note: When done properly, most of the oil should still be in the pan.

Grilled Tofu

This is a simple technique to impart flavor into your tofu dish. The marinade is for one pound of tofu cut into three slabs.

Basic Marinade

½ cup olive oil
¼ cup tamari soy sauce
1 tablespoon black pepper

For variations, add mustard, BBQ sauce, lime, honey or agave, or Cajun Spice (see *Common Ingredients* that follows for the spice blend recipe).

Procedure

Let the tofu sit in the marinade for at least 20 to 30 minutes. Then, on a hot grill with very clean grates, gently lay the tofu slabs down and leave them for about 3 minutes. Then turn the tofu one-quarter turn to create crisscrossed grill marks and cook another 2 minutes. Then, brush the top of the tofu with the marinade and flip it. Brush the already grilled side (now face up) with the marinade again and let it sit for 3 to 4 minutes.

Working with Seitan

Seitan, more than anything else, is what brings customers into Horizons Café. Seitan is a lot easier to prepare than tofu, and you could practically eat it right out of the package if you so wanted. It takes on meat-like textures and flavors that make it such a convenient steppingstone into meatless cuisine. Essentially, seitan is wheat gluten. All flour is made up of starch and gluten. By washing all the starch out of your flour, you are left with just gluten, which is then simmered in a flavorful stock to become seitan.

Seitan is a super food. It's practically fat free, very low in carbohydrates, and loaded with protein. It also does a marvelous job of substituting the hearty, meaty protein portions for which many vegetarians long and to which meat eaters are so accustomed. At the restaurant, we grill seitan steaks, sear BBQ wings, stuff filets with mushrooms and bake them with a pecan-sage crust…just to name a few of its many uses.

It was my sisters who first introduced me to seitan. They brought some to Thanksgiving for me to try one year when we were young. Unfortunately, it wasn't prepared very well. If I remember correctly, it was baked plain. Needless to say, it was not very tasty. However, like with tofu, I saw its potential and started to cook with it in every way that I knew how. With seitan, the results should come easily to you, and your family and guests will be truly impressed by it.

When you purchase it, you will get a mixed bag of scraps, chunks, and maybe a steak, if you're lucky. We offer a variety of recipes for all different sized cuts of seitan. Regardless of the different methods of preparation, there are some basic tips that you should always follow when working with seitan. The first thing you want to do when you buy it is drain and wash off the liquid in which it was packed. If you don't use it all right away, try a new recipe the next night; it perishes rapidly. I've included recipes within this cookbook, such as soups and seitan "chicken salad," that are opportune ways to use up all the little bits and scraps that you will accumulate when using seitan. You can also freeze all the little bits and then take them out to use when you have enough to make one of the "scrap" recipes. Seitan scraps are also terrific in spaghetti sauce, sloppy joes, and tacos.

Basic Cooking Methods

Whether you plan to make tofu, seitan, mushrooms, vegetables, or a whole meal, below are some basic cooking methods that you will use when preparing the savory recipes found within this cookbook. For cooking methods regarding baked goods, refer the *Desserts* section for more information.

Grilling

This is my all-time favorite preparation method with the jumping flames, the char marks on juicy zucchini or meaty mushrooms, the smoky essences on tomatoes and Belgian endive—and, oh—the peppers and onions!

To grill, you need just a little oil. Most of it burns off, and you're left with wonderful flavor. The type of grill you use makes a big difference. If you are using an outdoor BBQ grill, the racks tend to be high up off the flames, and the marks you get may not be very defined. I like to keep my outdoor grill on very high heat, allowing it to heat for about 10 minutes before putting anything on it. If some of you are lucky enough to have an indoor grill, you will notice that the flames are much closer to the grates, and your grill marks will be more defined. Whatever you do, make sure that when you lay something on a grill rack, you leave it sit for a few minutes to start to cook. If you try to turn it right away, it will stick.

I don't recommend grill pans or indoor electric grills because they lack the authentic grill flavor. If you must use them, they will work, but keep in mind that some flavor will be sacrificed because of the absence of the flames.

Measuring

One of the reasons that I have always despised cookbooks is the fact that they rely on measuring to the point where the techniques and knowledge of ingredients and their properties are lost underneath the tablespoons and behind the cups. I decided that if I was going to do a cookbook, I was going to try to teach people *how* to cook. This is art—not science. I think that it's important to come away from each recipe with knowledge of the technique that you just completed. You can always say "Yeah, I did it," but what is most important is being able to say, "I learned how to do it."

Roasting

Roasting is a fantastic way to bring out the deep flavors from within your foods. This is a great indoor, rustic way of cooking. When roasting vegetables, you'll need a little oil on them first or they will shrivel up and dry out. I like roasting most vegetables on high heat and charring the edges so they stay juicy inside. When roasting vegetables, such as onions, garlic and, peppers, you can also cook them on low heat with some oil for a long period of time to bring out all their natural sugars. They will come out soft and sweet—good enough to eat on their own. The broiler in your oven is a wonderful way to get last-minute color on something before you serve it.

Sautéing

Sautéing is a classic—mushrooms in wine sauce, greens in garlic and oil, pan-seared tofu…. Like an old black-and-white movie, this is what has been done so well for so long. Sautéing is not just letting something cook in a fry pan. It is an art! Don't think this is a saucepot or stew; sautéing relies as much on timing as grilling does. *Sauter* means "to jump" in French; this explains the high heat and quick cooking. You have to stay with your pan from start to finish, making sure the oil is at the right temperature and that you don't burn or overcook your food. To know how to sauté is to be a good cook. We will show you when to add your wine, how to keep your garlic from burning, and how to make sure your sauce is just right in the end.

Chef Rich conjures up some dancing flames as he grills a seitan steak for a Horizons Café customer

Common Ingredients for Savory Foods

. . . .

Beans

Beans are the foundation of many cuisines in the world—red beans in Mexico and Jamaica, black beans from Cuba to Brazil, and every other imaginable bean found in between. I use beans for their textures and flavors to complement a dish. I have adapted the cookbook recipes to use canned beans. There is no shame in it, and your results will be decent enough without all the trouble of having to soak and cook dried beans. Just remember to drain the packing liquid from the can and rinse the beans thoroughly. If you want to make beans from scratch, you will be rewarded for it with extra flavor. I always recommend soaking the beans overnight, rather than trusting any quick-soak methods prescribed on a package. You can find more information on beans in the *Soups* section.

Citrus

Have dinner at Horizons Café and, most likely, your dish will be garnished with a wedge of citrus: lemon for Mediterranean-inspired dishes and lime for Latin-inspired dishes. A last-minute squeeze of citrus is a birth rite. It brings out all the flavors and lightens up everything. In a recipe, citrus juice is an irreplaceable source of acidity.

Corn

Corn is all over Horizons cuisine. I love the stuff—sweet in flavor, bright white or yellow in color, and, as far as texture goes, you just can't beat the fresh crunch of good corn. I have based these recipes around frozen corn for convenience. It is one vegetable that freezes extremely well, and when it thaws, it retains its color and sweet flavor. If you want to use fresh corn, I highly encourage you to do so. At the restaurant, we shuck it, boil if for 3 to 4 minutes, brush it with a little oil, lightly grill it to add a smoky flavor, and then cut it right off the cob with a knife.

Cream Cheese (Soy)

You will find soy cream cheese as an ingredient in many recipes. Rather than rely on oil to make a foundation on which to carry your flavors, soy cream cheese is an excellent, creamy canvas that thickens and adds a wonderful silkiness to soups and sauces. If you don't want to use soy cream cheese, you can substitute the measured equivalent of raw tofu instead, but be sure that the tofu cooks a bit longer to minimize the soy taste.

Fructose

For these cookbook recipes, fructose is the sweetener of choice. It has many of the qualities of cane sugar, but it is much easier on your bloodstream, meaning that you aren't left feeling the extreme highs and lows after ingesting it. The purpose of using a sweetener in savory food is not to add sweetness, rather it is used to lightly balance the acidic flavors often added such as wine, mustard, vinegar, and citrus.

If you are a diehard sugar fan, all of these recipes are easily adapted by substituting sugar for fructose at a one-to-one ratio. You might also want to try turbinado sugar or raw cane sugar—two options that are less processed than white sugar. Lastly, guarapo (pressed sugarcane juice) is another excellent sweetener for savory food. While little Cuban take-out shacks in Miami seem to have no problem serving it as a beverage, fresh-pressed guarapo is hard to find in the Northeast. If you can get your hands on some, guarapo is superb in any Latin-inspired recipes.

Ginger

Usually referred to as *gingerroot*, this is a rhizome, which is an underground stem. Don't limit ginger to Asian cooking—it grows all over the tropics. It's an amazing, unique, and irreplaceable flavor. Ginger must be peeled first. Be careful when cutting it. It has a "grain," and you should always cut with the grain.

Hearts of Palm

Hearts of palm can be found inside the Palmito (or Cabbage Palm) tree. It's an excellent, exotic ingredient to include in your tropical cuisine. If you can find them fresh, by all means, pay any price—they are phenomenal. Most likely, the hearts of palm you do find will be in a can or jar, either from Costa Rica or Brazil. The hearts of palm we use at the restaurant come in a plastic-lined can from Guyana on the North Coast of South America. I have met the people who run Native Forest™, and they were very proud to tell me about their methods of organic and sustainable farming where they go to great lengths to reharvest each tree rather than destroy the whole crop per harvest.

Herbs

In my view, the difference between dry and fresh herbs is extreme. They should be used in completely different applications and treated as completely different food items as we describe in more detail in the Soups section.

I only use dry herbs as a flavor foundation when I begin to cook a sauce or soup. Dried herbs will dissipate their flavor all throughout the cooking process.

On the other hand, fresh herbs are what makes cooking magical. Buy them fresh and buy them often. Keep little pots in your kitchen window, sprigs in a vase of water, or, better yet, plants in your garden. They are inexpensive and most varieties are easy to grow. They will take your cooking to new heights. Chopped fresh herbs should be used when finishing a dish (last minute). Let them turn bright green and let loose their magic powers. Garnish with them too, since the steam from your meal will release the herb's aromas. You also can take that stick of rosemary, thyme, or tarragon, and brush it on your potatoes, seitan, or mushrooms to add that last explosion of fresh flavor.

Mayo, Vegan Mayo

There are several types of vegan mayonnaise on the market these days, but I love Vegenaise® with the blue label. Recipes that call for mayo in this cookbook have been built around this brand. Like a traditional mayonnaise, it is heavy, so use it in moderation.

Mustard

I must admit to being a huge mustard fan, and I love all mustards. However, when it comes to cooking, I swear by high-quality Dijon mustards. Spend the money, buy a great top-of-the-line Dijon, and it will pay you back in gastronomic pleasure. Mustard adds body to salad dressings and sauces without adding any fat. Its acidity can be balanced with other flavors and maybe a touch of sweetener.

Oil

My oil of choice is a Canola-and-Virgin-Olive-Oil blend, available in most supermarkets. For Horizons cuisine, it provides the perfect balance between the durability of Canola oil needed to cook on high heat and the rich flavors of olive oil that add to the overall taste of a dish. In your culinary explorations, however, you will most certainly want to use different oils for different purposes. Here are a few random tips about different oils:

- **Extra Virgin Olive Oil** - One of my favorite food ingredients, Extra Virgin Olive Oil is the first pressing of the olives, and the flavor is unbelievable. Buy small bottles, and buy them often. You will loose its very expensive flavor if you use it for cooking. Only add it to appropriate salad dressings and a drizzle to finish a dish.

- **Virgin Olive Oil** - Virgin Olive Oil is the second pressing of the olives. It is more affordable and you still get a good deal of flavor.

- **Pomace and Pure Olive Oil** - The third and fourth pressing of olives, these oils are lighter in flavor, but also good for cooking.

- **Light Olive Oil** - Don't be fooled by the term "light" olive oil; this only refers to the color and flavor, not the fat content. All oil has 14 grams of fat per tablespoon.

- **Canola Oil** - A cousin of ancient rapeseed oil from Asia, this oil is extremely durable for cooking on high heat, but it lacks flavor.

- **Flavorful Oils** - You will also see flavorful oils in this cookbook, such as peanut oil or toasted sesame oil. They are excellent ways to get flavor while cooking with fat, and a little goes a long way.

Rice

Rice is a great world-cuisine staple—aromatic jasmine and basmati, nutty wild wehani and japonica. Rice is a superb foundation of a good meal. See pages 91-94 for some of my favorite recipes, which can be used with wild, brown, white or whatever type of rice you may like.

The secret to cooking perfect rice is to follow the proportions needed (all my recipes are written for two cups of uncooked rice). If you don't like starchy/sticky rice, then rinse your rice in a strainer first, before cooking. Also, never rely on the cooking time indicated on a package. Stoves are different and people's interpretation of low, medium, and high heat vary. Check the rice for doneness about 5 to 10 minutes before the package claims it will be done. I like to pull my rice off the stove at a point where it is just underdone to my taste. This is where the culinary term "carry-over cooking" comes into play. The rice will keep cooking, so if you aren't going to serve it right away, spread it out loosely on a baking tray to let it cool. Then, reheat in a microwave before serving.

Salt

Very simply put, salt is the best way to enhance existing flavors. We never use salt to make a dish "salty," rather we use just enough to make flavors recognizable.

Soy Sauce, Tamari

Soy sauce is a generalization, and when you buy an inexpensive product, which is simply labeled "soy sauce," you are doing your cooking a huge injustice. Tamari is a fermented soybean liquid that is full of exotic, mysterious flavor. Buy quality soy sauce, just like you would a good red wine or single malt scotch. Tamari is the Japanese version, which is my choice, although shoyou, which is the Chinese version, is perfectly acceptable. Yes, they are salty, but when you buy a quality tamari or shoyou and use it properly, you get a rich, dark depth of flavor.

Spices

Spices are the aromatic-wonder ingredients that make a flavor foundation in your cooking. Don't keep spices too long; their pungency will fade. Buy them in small containers, and buy them often. Use dashes here and there to add interesting dimension to your sauces and soups. Spices should be very subtle on the palate. For instance, I love cumin, but I don't want to really taste it in my final dish. It should be supporting and enhancing the other ingredients, not dominating them. Like dry herbs, spices need to cook to dissipate their flavor.

I especially love Latin spices, like achiote, paprika, cumin, coriander, and allspice. I also love curry powder blends. I think I've tried almost every brand on the market and some that aren't.

Throughout this book you will see "Cajun or Southwest spice blend" or "jerk or tropical-spice blend." We custom blend our spices at the restaurant, and the following recipes are very similar to what we use. If you don't want to go to the trouble of mixing them, by all means, buy a pre-blended mix from the market. Just make sure that salt isn't the first ingredient, which is usually the sign of a lower-quality mix. You can use these market mixes, but make sure that you adjust you salt accordingly throughout the rest of the recipe that you are making.

Cajun Spice

1 tablespoon paprika
1 tablespoon cumin
1 tablespoon granulated onion
1 tablespoon granulated garlic
1 tablespoon salt
1 tablespoon black pepper
2 teaspoons thyme
2 teaspoons oregano
¼ teaspoon clove
½ teaspoon allspice
¼ teaspoon cayenne pepper (optional)

Island Spice

1 tablespoon paprika
1 tablespoon cumin
1 tablespoon granulated onion
1 tablespoon granulated garlic
1 tablespoon salt
1 tablespoon black pepper
1 teaspoon nutmeg
½ teaspoon clove
1 teaspoon ground ginger
2 teaspoons allspice
2 teaspoons thyme
2 teaspoons fructose or brown sugar

Stock, Vegetable

A good vegetable broth is an absolute key component in good cooking. Remember that the stockpot is not a garbage pail; onion skins and carrot tops belong in your compost pile—not your broth. What immediately follows is a recipe for making your own, but in this book, I recommend finding a cube, powder, or package of mix that you like. Just remember one very important thing: make your vegetable broth first, and then taste it. It should be good enough to eat as a soup on its own. If that's the case, then you are ready to begin. If your vegetable stock is not right, adjust it by adding more or less concentrate. Never start a recipe with a product that you will have to fix down the line.

Ingredients

2 tablespoons canola oil
1 large onion, roughly chopped
4 large carrots, roughly chopped
1 stalk celery without leaves (the leaves are bitter)
2 parsnips, roughly chopped
1 portabella mushroom (optional, will make a darker, richer stock)
4 garlic cloves
2 quarts water
¼ teaspoon tumeric
2 dry bay leaves
1 teaspoon salt, more to taste
1 bunch fresh thyme
1 bunch fresh parsley
1 pound spinach
1 bunch asparagus bottoms (bottom third of stalks)

Note: By roasting most of the vegetables first, you get a head start on flavor. If you don't have as much time and you want to bypass that step, save yourself from dirtying an extra pan by starting your vegetables in 2 tablespoons of very hot canola oil at the bottom of your stock pot. Then after they sizzle in the oil for 5 minutes, add the water.

To roast your vegetables, preheat the oven to 500°. Arrange the onion, carrot, celery, parsnip, portabella, and garlic on a roasting tray. Drizzle with 2 tablespoons of olive or canola oil, and roast for 7 to 8 minutes. Then, add the vegetables to the stockpot with the water, tumeric, and bay leaves. Bring to a boil. Add the salt and simmer for 20 minutes.

Next, add the thyme, parsley, spinach and asparagus. Simmer for 3 to 4 minutes, or until the spinach turns very bright green. Don't let it overcook, or it will become gray in color and will make the stock bitter.

Drain the stock into another pot or a bowl through a colander or large sieve. Discard the cooked vegetables. Return stock to a simmer and reduce contents by about one-third to concentrate the flavor. Now, you may add a splash of wine for extra fragrance. Check the stock to see if you would like to add more salt. If your stock is weak or watery, continue to reduce it to about half of the original volume. You may freeze the stock if you don't plan to use it within 3 days.

Wine

It's amazing how cooking with wine can take your dishes to new levels. Even if you don't drink alcohol, don't be afraid to cook with a little wine. It's not about the alcohol, which cooks off anyway in a matter of seconds. What you are left with is the essence of the fermented grape, and it does wonders and adds sophistication to your dish.

When cooking with wine, it is important to use a decent brand. You don't need the best wine in the world to cook, but we all know that we shouldn't cook with wine that we wouldn't drink. You can get a nice bottle of white wine, like Chardonnay or Sauvignon Blanc, for $7 or $8. You also can get a suitable bottle of red wine, like Cabernet Sauvignon or Merlot, for about $10.

In some recipes, I suggest fortified wines, like sherry, Marsala, and Madeira. The fermenting ends prematurely for these wines, leaving powerful natural sugars and flavors to add greater depth to your dish. Just remember, every wine should be reduced to concentrate the flavor and to cook off the alcohol content. If you are using a very high-quality wine, you can add a few drops at the last second before serving to brighten your dish and take it over the top.

Soups

. . . .

Soup, I believe, is the great common denominator food of the planet. Each culture seems to have its own signature soup: bouillabaisse in France, sopa de tortilla in Mexico, miso in Japan, callaloo in the Caribbean, black bean in Cuba, etc.

Soup satisfies on such a deeper level. The poetic motion of a spoon being lifted from a steaming soup bowl to one's mouth is almost spiritual. When you are cold or ill, a bowl of hot soup represents all that is right and good in the world.

Every morning in the restaurant (sometimes in the afternoon too), that's what I do: I make soup, and I love doing it. My favorite aspect about our soup is that I may be out somewhere, and I will read a menu (an obsessive habit) and see something that looks so good, but I don't want to eat it because of animal products—whether it be a soup or an entrée of some sort. So I go into work the next day and make a "horizonized" soup out of it for all of us to enjoy.

Beans in Soup

To make these recipes easier, I've based them around canned beans, which I feel work just fine in a soup that is flavored and prepared properly. If you would like to use dried beans, they require a bit of extra work, but it will pay off in flavor. Remember to sort through the dried beans to look for pebbles and such. Soak your beans for at least 2 hours, but preferably overnight. Cook black beans in their soaking liquid to retain that deep, dark black broth. For all other beans, discard the soaking water and start with fresh water about 2 to 3 inches above the beans. Bring them to a boil, and then simmer until tender.

Remember, when cooking your dried beans, to season with a little of the herbs and spices to be used later on in the recipe! This will give your beans a nice foundation of flavor. Be careful with the salt, which will keep your beans from cooking properly if used too early. Add it about three-quarters of the way through the cooking time.

Herbs

I much prefer dried herbs in the beginning of the soup because of their slow dissipation of flavor. Fresh herbs are best used at the very end of the soup for a final burst of flavor. However, you will not get the flavor-layering effect that dried herbs will give you in the beginning. Also, leafy fresh herbs will quickly lose their green brilliance and end up a pale gray.

The best-case scenario is to use the recommended dried herbs in the beginning and then stir in a little of their fresh versions right before the soup is served.

Roasted Vegetable Gazpacho with Avocado Aioli

Whenever we make gazpacho in the restaurant, it's gone before you know it. There's just something special about a chilled soup on a hot day. Kate always talks so fondly about the gazpachos she had in Spain...and the way they were served with chopped cucumbers and bread on the side. This inspired me to create this recipe. Roasting the vegetables brings out so much flavor, and the creamy avocado aioli is a nice, smooth balance.

Ingredients for Gazpacho

10 plum tomatoes, halved
1 onion, chunked
5 garlic cloves
1 poblano or red bell pepper
2 carrots
½ cup olive oil
¼ cup red wine
1 teaspoon salt
1 teaspoon black pepper
1 tablespoon paprika
1 teaspoon ground cumin
1 tablespoon fructose or agave nectar
2 cucumbers, peeled and seeded
12 ounces carrot or tomato juice
½ cup fresh herbs of your choice, such as
    cilantro, parsley, thyme, or basil

Ingredients for Avocado Aioli

2 ripe avocados
1 garlic clove
½ cup vegan mayo
½ teaspoon salt
½ teaspoon pepper
1 lime, juiced
1 jalapeno, no seeds or stems (optional)
1 tablespoon fresh cilantro, chopped (optional)

Yields: 10 to 12 servings

See photo on page 59

On a large roasting tray arrange the tomatoes, onion, garlic cloves, bell pepper, and carrots. Drizzle with the olive oil and pour the red wine into the bottom of the pan. Sprinkle with salt, pepper, paprika, cumin, and fructose. Roast at 500° for about 20 minutes or until the tomato skins blister.

When finished, purée the roasted mixture in a food processor with the cucumbers, carrot juice, and chosen fresh herbs. If you'd like, add more fresh, chopped vegetables; such as tomato, bell pepper, green onion, etc. Then, chill the gazpacho for at least 30 minutes.

For the aioli topping, place all of the avocado aioli ingredients in a food processor or blender and process until creamy and smooth. This should be done as close to serving time as possible to minimize the avocado oxidation, which will make the aioli turn gray.

When ready to serve, place the gazpacho in individual serving bowls or cups and top each with a dollop of avocado aioli.

Cajun Lentil Soup with Vegetarian Sausage

Cajun food doesn't have to be very spicy—just full of flavor...and that is what this soup is all about! The sausage is an earthy and meaty touch. It's a nice soup to come home to after a colder-than-expected day (like the ones I had when visiting New Orleans). Ideally, lentils should be soaked for about an hour, but if you don't have the time, that's OK, just use the red lentils since they won't need presoaking. I like red lentils because they are colorful and break down to make a creamy consistency. Green lentils don't have much of an appearance before or after cooking, but their shape holds better if you like a chunkier soup.

Ingredients

2 quarts stock
1 teaspoon salt and pepper
¾ pound red or green lentils
2 tablespoons Creole or Cajun Spice blend
    (see the *Getting Started* section)
½ onion, chopped
2 garlic cloves, minced
2 stalks celery, chopped
½ red bell pepper, chopped
Canola or olive oil
8 ounces vegetarian sausage links or patties
½ tablespoon ketchup
Hot sauce

Yields: 10 to 12 servings

See photo on page 58

Season the cooking stock with the salt and pepper. Cook the lentils until they are tender (about 20 minutes for red lentils and about 45 minutes for the green lentils).

Halfway through the cooking process, add 1 tablespoon of the Creole or Cajun Spice blend. Also add the onion, garlic, celery and red bell pepper, and let it simmer for 10 minutes. *Note*: If you prefer a stronger flavor, you can first roast the chopped vegetables in a little olive oil under your oven broiler for 6 to 7 minutes before adding them to the soup.

In a skillet, cook the vegetarian sausage links or patties in a little oil (or CTF by heating them in a microwave). Coarsely chop the sausage in a food processor or by hand. Add the chopped sausage to the soup, along with the ketchup, as it nears completion.

Re-season the soup with the second tablespoon of the Creole or Cajun Spice blend. Add a couple dashes, or as much as you would like, of the hot sauce. I'd even recommend as much as ⅛ cup!

Lastly, if you opted to cook the sausage in oil, and if you don't mind a little extra fat, make sure you add that cooking oil to the soup—they wouldn't have it any other way down in Louisiana!

Creamy Carrot Soup

Anguilla is a flat, arid island in the Northern Caribbean. Most people day trip there from the French side of Saint Martin. I did the opposite. While there, I discovered this incredible soup—creamy carrots touched so perfectly with Caribbean spices. As soon as I got back, it became a Horizon standby and is one of my favorites. The puréed carrots give the impression of a very thick and luxurious soup.

Ingredients

2 quarts stock

2 pounds carrots, peeled and chopped
   (rough chop all the vegetables because this soup will be puréed)

½ onion, chopped

2 garlic cloves, chopped

2 teaspoon fresh ginger, chopped

½ teaspoon cumin

½ teaspoon allspice

½ teaspoon nutmeg

½ tub soy cream cheese
   (CTF by using only ¼ of the tub)

1 cup coconut milk

Yields: 10 to 12 servings

See photo on page 59

Start your stock pot. Boil the carrots in the stock for about 8 minutes. Add the other vegetables, herbs, spices, and cream cheese. Boil for another 5 minutes, and then add the coconut milk.

Purée the entire soup, about two cups at a time, in a good, strong blender until smooth. Be very careful when puréeing hot liquids! The heat and steam can cause the contents to burst out from beneath the lid. Always begin by pulsing the blender gradually, and then move to a steady purée. Add more stock, coconut milk, or water to get the consistency you desire. (I like mine a bit on the thin side, but it is great very thick as well.)

Variation: Try replacing some of the carrots with sweet potatoes, squash, or corn kernels when you begin boiling the carrots.

Vegetarian Manhattan Clam Chowder

Anyone who has spent some time in any coastal-port town will know the importance of seafood to that community. Seafood chowders are found everywhere from take-out shacks to fine restaurants. This recipe is a convincing vegetarian seafood soup, using all traditional ingredients (except the seafood of course), and it is my absolute favorite. As a side note, some seafood seasonings can be very spicy or salty, so be sure to check them before starting in case you need to adjust the salt.

Ingredients

2 quarts stock
2 carrots, diced
2 celery stalks, diced
1 small onion, diced
2 medium sized potatoes, diced
2 or 3 garlic cloves, minced
2 teaspoons dried thyme
1 teaspoon granulated garlic
1 teaspoon granulated onion
1 teaspoon dried oregano
2 tablespoons seafood seasoning
8 ounces canned diced tomatoes
16 ounces tomato purée
1 cup textured soy protein (TSP) granules
½ cup white wine or sherry
2 tablespoon fructose
2 tablespoons olive oil
     (CTF by not using any oil)
Salt and pepper to taste

Yields: 10 to 12 servings

Start your stock pot and add the carrots, celery, onion, potatoes, garlic, and thyme. Bring to boil.

Add the granulated garlic, granulated onion, oregano, 1 tablespoon of the seafood seasoning, diced tomatoes, and tomato purée. Bring to boil.

Add the TSP granules, white wine, fructose, and oil. Bring to boil again.

Reduce heat and simmer until the potatoes are tender. Finish with the second tablespoon of seafood seasoning and the salt and pepper.

Red Bean & Bacon Soup

I saw this soup on the "specials" board at one of my favorite restaurants in Key West. It sounded like such a good flavor combination that I just had to Horizonize it for our guests back home. I think you'll like the results. The red kidney beans have a more dramatic effect, but I prefer the creaminess of the pinto beans.

Ingredients

2 quarts stock

½ onion, diced

2 garlic cloves, minced

1 large carrot, diced the size of the beans

2 tablespoons Cajun Spice blend (see the *Getting Started* **section)**

2 (15-ounce) cans of red kidney or pinto beans, drained and rinsed

½ cup uncooked jasmine or other white rice

¼ cup sherry

2 tablespoons canola or olive oil

1 package vegetarian bacon or ham

Salt and pepper to taste

Yields: 10 to 12 servings

Bring your stock pot to a boil with the onion, fresh garlic, and carrot. Add the Cajun Spice blend and simmer for 5 minutes to create a flavor foundation. Add the beans, rice, and sherry. Bring the mixture to a simmer and cook about 10 minutes.

Meanwhile, in a skillet, heat the oil and pan fry your favorite brand of vegetarian bacon (vegetarian ham works well too). Set the fried bacon on paper towels to remove the excess oil.

Cut the bacon into julienne strips or small pieces. Add the bacon to the soup's last minutes of cooking, along with salt and pepper.

Provençal White Bean Soup

I love using white beans in French food. They are a great canvas for painting colors and flavors. This soup brings out some of the great classic tastes of France. The herbs, tomatoes, and garlic are all hallmarks of Southern French cuisine. Celeriac is an unusual vegetable that is starting to catch on. It's the root from the celery seed plant, and it has a nice rounded, earthy flavor. I think it compliments the beans wonderfully in this soup.

Ingredients

2 quarts stock
½ small onion, finely chopped
½ celeriac, peeled and chopped about the same size as the beans
2 garlic cloves, minced
½ tablespoon Dijon mustard
¼ cup sherry
¼ cup white wine
2 (15-ounce) cans of white navy or great northern beans, drained and rinsed
1 tablespoon fresh thyme
½ tablespoon fresh parsley
½ teaspoon fresh tarragon
Salt and pepper to taste
1 tablespoon extra virgin olive oil
1 red tomato; diced, salted, and drained (see *Tip*)

Yields: 10 to 12 servings

Bring your stock pot to a boil with the onion, celeriac, and garlic. Add the Dijon mustard, sherry, and white wine, and bring to a boil again.

Next, add the beans and simmer for 5 minutes so the flavors mingle, then add the fresh herbs, salt, pepper, olive oil (CTF by not adding any), and tomato.

Tip: Here's a great little trick for waking up your tomatoes. Dice them, toss them with a few sprinkles of salt, and leave them in a strainer for 30 minutes. The tomatoes will release a lot of their water and taste phenomenal.

Tofu Crab & Corn Bisque

Growing up in Philadelphia means you are full of warm, wonderful childhood memories of the Jersey shore. We always took for granted that we were a mere hour from the coast and that most of the country does not enjoy this privilege. Here's a cleaned up version of the soup that everyone has seen, smelled, and/or tasted in most Jersey-shore restaurants—Seafood Bisque.

Ingredients

2 quarts stock
1 (16-ounce) can crushed tomatoes or tomato purée
1 cup roasted red peppers (canned or jarred), puréed
1 small green pepper, minced
¼ cup onion, minced
2 cups corn kernels (fresh or frozen)
1 teaspoon granulated garlic
1 teaspoon granulated onion
1 teaspoon dried thyme
1 teaspoon dried oregano
1 tablespoon fructose
½ teaspoon crushed fennel seed (optional)
2 to 3 saffron strands
1 cup tofu, diced (see *Variation*)
1 tablespoon seafood seasoning
1 tub soy cream cheese (CTF by using only half of the tub)
¼ cup flour
1 cup sherry
Salt and pepper to taste

Yields: 10 to 12 servings

Begin your stock pot with the tomatoes and red-pepper purée. Add the green pepper, onion, and corn as well as the granulated garlic, granulated onion, thyme, and oregano. Bring to a boil.

Next, stir in the fructose, fennel, and saffron. Bring to a boil again. Add the tofu and seafood seasoning and simmer for 5 minutes.

Meanwhile, in a blender, purée the soy cream cheese, flour, and sherry until smooth and creamy. If this mixture is too thick, add some of the stock pot liquid to thin it while you purée.

When finished, add the creamy mixture from the blender and allow to thicken by bringing it to a boil. Add salt and pepper.

Variation: Instead of adding the plain, diced tofu to the soup mixture, roast it first on a baking sheet with 2 tablespoons of oil, 1 teaspoon seafood seasoning, and ¼ cup white wine. It's one extra step that makes a significant difference.

Sea Vegetable Soup with Asian Greens & Ginger

Sea vegetables are interesting things. Literally seaweed, they are full of great flavor and nutrition. I recommend wakame for its delicate flavor and texture. The soup finishes with the familiar nori, or sushi seaweed, which gives it a wonder aromatic flavor of the sea. Make a light meal out of it by adding rice noodles or basmati rice!

Ingredients

2 quarts stock

2 tablespoons ginger, grated

2 garlic cloves, minced

1 leek (or 1 small onion), chopped

1 celery stalk, diced

½ cup dried wakame seaweed, soaked in water
and then chopped

1 tablespoon arrowroot powder or cornstarch

½ tablespoon sesame oil

1 tablespoon tamari soy sauce

Black or white pepper

1 sheet of nori, cut into strips

2 cups chopped Asian greens (bok choy, nappa
cabbage, or even spinach work well)

1 to 2 teaspoons wasabi or red chile paste
(optional)

¼ cup scallions, chopped

Yields: 10 to 12 servings

Bring your stock pot to a boil with the ginger, garlic, leek, and celery. Add the wakame seaweed and bring to a boil again.

In the meantime, blend the arrowroot powder, sesame oil, and tamari in a small mixing boil with just enough water to make a smooth, milky consistency.

Slowly stir in the contents of the small mixing bowl into the stock pot. Bring to a boil and then remove from heat, stirring in the black or white pepper, nori, and Asian greens. Also add the red chile paste or wasabi (or both) if you desire. Stir in the scallions just before serving.

Tortilla Soup with Roasted Seitan

A Mexican tradition is sopa de tortilla, which is a tomato-based soup with strips of fried tortillas on top. It's served with condiments on the side, such as cilantro, avocado, and sour cream. We do an entrée version at the restaurant with grilled seitan and a green chile broth. This version is full of vegetables, so it's more like a Mexican beef stew. Add some tortilla right into the soup to thicken it and also place some on top as garnish.

Ingredients

2 quarts stock

2 cups vegetable trinity, diced
(equal parts celery, bell pepper & onion)

1 cup fresh or frozen corn kernels

12 to 16 ounces chopped seitan, browned with
1 tablespoon olive or canola oil

1 tablespoon garlic, minced

2 tablespoons Southwest or Cajun Spice blend
(see the *Getting Started* section)

1 chile pepper, chopped (optional)

½ cup cooked rice

1 cup tomato, diced

1 ripe avocado, diced

Tortilla chips or strips (red & blue chips add an
interesting contrast)

Yields: 10 to 12 servings

See photo on page 60

Bring your stock pot to a boil with the vegetable trinity, corn, browned seitan, and spices. Reduce heat and simmer for 5 minutes

Right before serving, add the rice, tomatoes, and avocado to the soup, and simmer for 2 more minutes; or if you prefer, serve the soup and top each bowl with the tomato, avocado, and rice. Garnish with tortillas and, if you wish, cilantro and sour cream.

Drunken Caribbean Black Bean Soup
with Vegan Mango Crema

Black beans are the base of so many Caribbean and South American foods. They take so well to the spices that are indigenous to the area. If you like a light, broth-based soup, don't purée it. Or if you prefer, you can purée half of the soup (that's the way I like it) for a rich and creamy version. This is one recipe where cooking with dried beans will make a huge difference.

Ingredients

1 pound black turtle beans, cooked

2 quarts stock

1 cup rum

½ onion, chopped

2 celery stalks, chopped

2 garlic cloves, minced

2 tablespoons Island Spice blend (see the *Getting Started* section)

1 (8-ounce) can regular or light coconut milk (CTF by using 2 teaspoons coconut extract or 12 ounces coconut juice)

Pulp of 1 ripe mango

2 tablespoons soy sour cream

2 teaspoons fresh cilantro, chopped

Lime slices (optional)

2 tablespoons diced red pepper (optional)

Yields: 10 to 12 servings

See photo on page 59

Soak the beans for at least 2 hours with water, covering the beans by about 3 inches. Then, on a low-simmering heat, start to cook the beans in their soaking liquid. After 20 minutes, add the stock. Simmer for another 20 minutes. Then, add the rum, vegetables, and spices, and continue to simmer.

When the beans are tender, stir in the coconut milk, and adjust the salt and pepper as necessary. If you need more liquid, add water; or if you believe that the beans taste weak, add more stock. The whole cooking process should take about 90 minutes.

If you're like me and prefer your black bean soup half puréed, put about 2 cups of soup in a blender and carefully pulse the contents of the blender at first so that the hot liquid does not splatter from beneath the lid. When finished, return the purée to the soup pot. You can also achieve the same result by using an immersion blender.

For the mango crema, combine the mango pulp and the soy sour cream in a blender and process until creamy.

Serve the soup hot, garnished with a dollop of chilled mango crema, the fresh chopped cilantro, a slice of lime, and some diced red pepper.

Tropical Seitan Beef Chowder

This soup is great with either seitan, tofu, textured soy protein (TSP) granules, or all three. It also a great way to use all those little seitan bits and scraps too. The coconut milk adds a nice canvas on which to paint tropical spices, such as nutmeg, allspice and clove. If you really want to go all out for a superb meal, try adding some calabaza (a Caribbean pumpkin squash, which is like butternut squash), or substitute the potatoes with boniatos (Cuban sweet potatoes), if you can find them. I love heat with coconut milk, so if you do too, add a chopped fresh hot chile pepper to the soup. Imagine that you are eating the chowder on a sand-floor restaurant near the water's edge. The flavors are so transporting that you'll want to send a postcard.

Ingredients

2 quarts stock

1 (12- to 15-ounce) can of coconut milk

2 potatoes, diced

2 celery stalks, diced

1 (12- to 15-ounce) can of crushed tomatoes
    or tomato purée

1 onion, diced

4 garlic cloves, crushed

24 ounces of seitan; rinsed, dried and chopped
    (substitute 1 pound of tofu or 1 cup TSP
    granules if you prefer)

2 tablespoons Tropical Spice blend (see the
    Getting Started section)

1 tablespoon freshly grated ginger

4 tablespoons fructose or brown sugar

¼ cup dark rum

½ cup dry jasmine rice

1 pinch saffron

Plantain or banana chips (optional)

*Yields: 4 servings as an entrée or 6 servings
    as a starter*

Put all ingredients in a large stockpot, bring to a boil, and then simmer for 15 more minutes. Serve with some plantain or banana chips.

Add some chopped mango or pineapple, or you can really spice it up authentically with a chopped habanero pepper (known as *Scotch Bonnett* in the Caribbean).

Irish Seitan Beef Stew

Has there ever been a country that is more captivating than Ireland? It's remarkably beautiful there with the green rolling hills , the enchanted forests, the charming villages, and the little pubs. Our memories from that voyage burn strong in me as does the Celtic culture. While the beer is topnotch, traditional Irish cuisine is not the most vegetarian-friendly in the world. One night in a pub, we indulged in some deep-fried mushrooms drenched in garlic butter. They were superb, but we are still, to this day, trying to get them out of our arteries. This soup, which is a take on traditional Irish beef stew, is my dedication to amazing Ireland.

Ingredients

2 quarts stock
2 potatoes, chopped
1 carrot, chopped
½ onion, chopped
2 garlic cloves, crushed
1 celery stalk, chopped
20 to 24 ounces seitan, rinsed and chopped
2 tablespoons fructose or brown sugar
12 ounces dark beer
1 tablespoon dried sage
1 tablespoon dried thyme
1 sprig fresh rosemary
1 tablespoon canola or olive oil

Yields: 10 to 12 servings

See photo on page 57

Put all ingredients in a large stockpot, bring to a boil, and then simmer for 15 more minutes. Pull out the rosemary sprig after 5 minutes and discard.

Variation: In a wok or thin sauté pan over high heat, brown the carrots, onion, seitan and potatoes in separate batches with 2 teaspoons of canola or olive oil each. The items will not cook through, rather the idea is to get some smoky flavor into your ingredients. The browning should take about 2 to 3 minutes for each batch. When completed, put all the ingredients in a stockpot, bring to a boil, and then simmer for 10 to 15 minutes.

Creamy Mushroom Soup with Rosemary

Mushrooms and rosemary were born for each other. Rosemary is one of my absolute favorite herbs. I love to get it fresh and just let the aroma take me away. Anyone who's been to Horizons knows that mushrooms rule; they show up everywhere. They are nature's meatless gift. Combine the two, and well...this soup is heavenly. You can use white mushrooms, but portabellas are amazing here. And, if it doesn't break the bank, chanterelle mushrooms take this recipe over the top.

Ingredients

2 quarts stock
2 pounds mushrooms, roughly chopped
   (these will be puréed later)
2 garlic cloves, crushed
2 shallots or ½ onion, chopped
½ cup white wine
½ tub soy cream cheese
   (CTF by using only ¼ tub)
1 teaspoon ground sage
1 teaspoon fructose
Dash nutmeg
2 tablespoons fresh rosemary leaves
2 tablespoons flour
Salt and pepper to taste

Yields: 10 to 12 servings

Boil the stock with the mushrooms. Add the garlic and shallots or onion. Add the white wine, soy cream cheese, ground sage, fructose, and nutmeg. Bring to a boil and then remove immediately from heat.

Add the fresh rosemary, flour, salt, and pepper. Be sure to add the flour very slowly so that it does not create lumps in the soup.

In a blender, two to four cups at a time, purée the entire soup. Remember to pulse the contents of the blender at first so that the hot liquid does not splatter from beneath the lid.

Return the puréed soup to the stove, and let it SLOWLY come to a simmer.

Pinto Bisque

In any world cuisine, especially Mexican, some of the most basic staples can create a sumptuous soup. Kate and I were recently on an eating tour in Miami when we had a soup just like this in a Mexican café.

Ingredients

2 quarts stock
2 cups onion, chopped
2 garlic cloves, chopped
½ red bell pepper, chopped
1 small tomato, chopped
1 teaspoon dried thyme
½ teaspoon cumin
½ teaspoon paprika
2 (15-ounce) cans of pinto beans,
    drained and rinsed
¼ cup sherry or tequila
Salt and pepper to taste
½ tub soy cream cheese or soy sour cream
    (CTF by using ¼ tub)

Yields: 10 to 12 servings

Begin by bringing your stock to a boil. Add the onions, garlic, red bell pepper, and tomato, and return to a boil. Add the thyme, cumin, and paprika. Allow to simmer for 5 minutes. Next, add the beans, sherry or tequila, soy cream cheese or sour cream, and return to a boil. Remove the soup from the heat.

In a blender, two cups at a time, purée the entire soup. Always take caution when blending hot liquids by pulsing the blender at first so as not to cause the liquid to squirt out from beneath the lid. When finished, return the purée to the cooking pot, and heat through for about 5 minutes.

Serve this soup simply and savor the creaminess; or, if you have them, serve it with some crushed tortilla chips to add a different texture. It's also great when topped with our Hearts of Palm, Mango & Avocado Salad (see page 52).

Feel Good Soup

If you're feeling under the weather, give this fiery soup a try. At the very least, it will clear your sinuses. Even if you aren't sick, but like spicy Asian foods, you'll love this combination of garlic, red chile, and wasabi. It's invigorating! The Feel Good Soup is more of a medicinal broth, but I've included options to make it more substantial.

Ingredients

1 tablespoon cooking oil
¼ cup onion, minced
¼ cup garlic, minced
¼ cup ginger, minced
2 quarts stock
1 tablespoon wasabi
1 tablespoon tamari soy sauce
½ teaspoon white pepper
1 tablespoon Korean or Thai red chile paste
1 teaspoon fructose
½ cup precooked rice
1 scallion, chopped for garnish

Yields: 10 to 12 servings

In a very hot wok, add your cooking oil. Brown the onion, garlic, and ginger, but don't let it burn.

Bring your stock to a boil in a large pot. Add the browned vegetables from the wok. Add the wasabi, tamari, white pepper, red chile paste, fructose, and rice to the boiling stock. Reduce the heat and keep the soup at a simmer for 5 minutes. Serve steaming hot with fresh scallions on top.

Variations: Try adding mushrooms to the wok mixture. Also, broccoli or finely chopped tofu works well as an addition. You also can substitute noodles for the rice. Lastly, if you prefer a thicker soup, thicken the broth with a slurry of 1 teaspoon arrowroot powder mixed with 2 tablespoons of cold broth or water. Stir it in during the last minute of cooking and allow to thicken slowly thicken.

Cauliflower & Grilled Green Onion Soup

Although cauliflower is not a spring vegetable, this soup just sings spring to me. You'll love the flavor that the grilled green onion imparts to this garden-inspired soup. Add soy cheese or potatoes if you want to expand on this recipe. Pita bread is a perfect complement.

Ingredients

2 tablespoon olive or canola oil
2 cups white onion, chopped
¼ cup garlic, chopped
1 teaspoon curry powder
1 tablespoon dried thyme
2 quarts stock
1 large , 2 small, or 1½ medium heads of
    cauliflower, roughly chopped
1 potato, chopped
1½ cups tofu
2 teaspoons fructose
Salt and pepper to taste
¼ cup Dijon mustard
3 bunches grilled green onions
    (brush with oil and grill for one minute
    until charred—these may also be done
    directly on an electric or gas burner)

Yields: 10 to 12 servings

Sauté the white onion and garlic in the oil for about 5 minutes or until translucent. Add the curry powder and thyme, and sauté for an additional minute so that the spices become aromatic.

Next, add the stock, sauté mixture, cauliflower, potato, tofu, fructose, salt, pepper and Dijon mustard to a large pot. Simmer for 15 minutes, until the cauliflower and potatoes are soft. Add the grilled green onions.

Purée with an immersion blender or in small batches in a regular blender. Use caution when blending hot liquids by pulsing the blender at first so as not to cause the liquid to squirt out from beneath the lid.

Return the puréed soup to the cooking pot, and simmer for 5 more minutes so that the flavors meld.

Creamy Butternut Squash & Carrot Soup

I did a Thanksgiving-themed cooking class for a natural foods store one year, and this recipe jumped right out at me as a perfect vegan lunch for the day of the big meal. Try this spirit-warming soup one day this November.

Ingredients

2 quarts stock
1 pound carrots, peeled and roughly chopped
1 butternut squash; seeds removed, peeled and chopped
1 block silken tofu
¼ cup white wine
2 teaspoons of canola or olive oil
2 garlic cloves, chopped
½ onion, chopped
1 teaspoon fresh ginger, chopped
½ teaspoon ground coriander
½ teaspoon ground allspice
Salt and pepper to taste
2 teaspoons olive oil

Yields: 10 to 12 servings

Boil all ingredients in a large stockpot for 10 minutes. If your carrots are not sweet, stir in a little fructose or sugar.

In a blender, two cups at a time, purée the entire soup. Use caution when blending hot liquids by pulsing the blender at first so as not to cause the liquid to squirt out from beneath the lid. Serve immediately.

Black Bean & Corn Soup with Vegetarian Sausage

A few years ago, I had ordered a vegetarian soup to go at a restaurant. After taking a big, blind, trusting spoonful, I realized it was not the soup that I had ordered, rather a pork sausage and bean soup. The restaurant owner, who is a friend of mine, was more upset than me. Anyway, I created this soup to erase my memory of the experience and to say, of course, we vegetarians can have this too!

Ingredients

2 quarts stock
1 tablespoon garlic, chopped
2 tablespoons Southwest or Cajun Spice blend
   (see the *Getting Started* section)
1 pound frozen corn
1 (15-ounce) can of black beans, rinsed
½ cup onion, chopped
½ cup bell pepper, chopped
½ cup celery, chopped
1 tablespoon canola or olive oil
1 package vegetarian sausage links

Yields: 10 to 12 servings

Bring your stock pot to a boil with the garlic, Southwest or Cajun Spice blend, corn, black beans, onion, bell pepper, and celery. Reduce the heat to a simmer.

Remove half of the soup pot's contents, and purée it in a blender by lightly pulsing. Use caution when blending hot liquids by pulsing the blender at first so as not to cause the liquid to squirt out from beneath the lid. Return the puréed mixture to the soup pot.

Using a sauté pan, cook your the vegetarian sausage links in olive oil until they are dark on the outside. Let cool slightly and then crumble. Add the sausage to the soup and heat another few minutes until it's at a good serving temperature.

Salads

. . . .

People are picky about salads. Some like to pour their dressing on, some like to dip, and some like their dressing tossed in. People know what they like when it comes to their salads. So here I offer you some ingredient combinations that work well with complimentary dressings. Use your favorite lettuce(s) as a base, and then paint your masterpiece with all of your favorite colors, flavors, and textures. Here's a basic mix:

- *Red Leaf and Romaine Lettuce as a base;*
- *Radicchio or Red Cabbage for color;*
- *Shredded Carrots for sweetness to balance out the radicchio or cabbage;*
- *Cucumbers, half peeled and seeds removed, for a fresh crunch;*
- *Red Radishes for color and texture; and*
- *Red Onion for its intense, raw flavor.*

Other possible ingredients include:

- *Belgian endive provides a striking and elegant presentation; although sometimes bitter, the leaves are artful and graceful.*
- *Chayote, a Mexican squash with a crisp, apple-like flesh, adds diversity for the tastebuds; cut into strips and add, skin and all.*
- *Mushrooms offer an earthy-textured salad accent; buy the whitest, freshest that you can find and slice them thin.*
- *Sprouts brighten up bitter lettuces; my favorites are sunflower sprouts, snow pea shoots, and the trusted alfalfa sprouts.*

Hearts of Palm, Jicama & Orange Salad with Lemon Cilantro Vinaigrette

Jicama is a root vegetable indigenous to Mexico. Its subtle, fresh flavor reminds me of a sort of radish. Make sure you cut off or peel the skin and cut the jicama into julienne strips. Hearts of palm are delicious tropical delicacies from the inside of the cabbage palm. It is almost impossible to find them fresh in the USA, but if you can, pay any price!!! They are worth it! Most other hearts of palm come from Costa Rica or Brazil in jars and cans. The jarred variety is far superior.

Ingredients for Salad

Oranges
Your choice of lettuce and vegetables
Hearts of palm
Jicima, julienned
Red bell pepper, julienned (optional)
Green or red onion, chopped (optional)

Ingredients for Lemon Cilantro Vinaigrette

1 large lemon, juiced
2 teaspoons good quality Dijon mustard
3 tablespoons rice wine vinegar
½ cup shallot or onion, finely minced
3 teaspoons fructose
Salt and pepper to taste
1 bunch fresh cilantro, finely chopped
¾ cup canola or olive oil
    (extra virgin olive oil is not recommended for this recipe)

Dressing Yields: 4 to 6 servings

See photo on page 62

Cut your oranges into wheels and peel the skin. Then, cut the wheels into halves or quarters and set aside.

Using a large bowl or plate, arrange your chosen lettuce and vegetable. Top with the hearts of palm, oranges, jicima as well as the red bell pepper and onions, if desired. Set aside.

In a mixing bowl, squeeze in the lemon juice. Add the Dijon mustard, rice wine vinegar, onion, fructose, salt, pepper, and cilantro. Whisk ingredients together. While whisking, drizzle in the oil.

Just before serving, spoon the vinaigrette dressing over the entire salad arrangement.

Avocado, White Bean & Smoked Tofu Salad
with Agave Mustard Vinaigrette

Here are some flavors that compliment each other so beautifully. Tofu takes on a cheesy-meaty texture. Buy your favorite brand of smoked tofu. Try to find Hass avocados from Mexico or California; they have a higher fat content than those from Florida, but it is well worth it. For the agave mustard, we take the traditional honey mustard dressing, give it a Southwest touch, and replace the honey with agave nectar (found in natural food stores). Agave nectar is a fructose-rich substance that is harvested from the blue agave cactus and works well as a substitute for honey.

Ingredients for Salad

Your choice of lettuce and vegetables
Canned white beans, drained and rinsed
Smoked tofu, cut into planks or cubes
Avocado, cut into planks or cubes
Black olives (optional)
Tortilla chips (optional)

Ingredients for Agave Mustard Vinaigrette

2 tablespoons agave nectar
2 teaspoons good quality Dijon Mustard
2 teaspoons Southwest or Cajun Spice blend
   (see the *Getting Started* section)
Salt to taste
1 small clove of garlic
2 teaspoons fresh onion, chopped
½ cup olive or canola oil

Dressing Yields: 4 to 6 servings

See photo on page 62

Using a large bowl or plate, arrange your lettuce and top with your choice of vegetables, the white beans, and the smoked tofu. Add the avocado and optional olives. Set aside.

In a blender, combine the agave nectar, Dijon mustard, spices, garlic clove, and onion and blend. While you continue to blend, drizzle in the oil until creamy.

Just before serving, spoon the vinaigrette dressing over the entire salad arrangement. Serve with tortilla chips for a nice texture contrast.

Radicchio, Watercress & Arugula Salad with a Baked Soy Cream Cheese Crostini & Balsamic Cranberry Vinaigrette

It's early October, a little wet and chilly, and you're psychologically preparing yourself for your autumn and winter journey. Here is fuel for your ship. I'm sure you will absolutely love this arrangement as it celebrates the season of just staying home. Please do not feel confined by the three lettuce leaves I have selected. Use a spring mix if you like or baby spinach or dark green romaine—use what you have and what you like!

Ingredients for Salad

French or Italian bread

Extra virgin olive oil (for baking)

Soy cream cheese

Black and white sesame seeds (optional)

Radicchio, watercress & arugula (or your
  choice of greens)

Fresh basil and parsley, chopped (optional)

Toasted walnuts or pine nuts (optional)

Ingredients for Balsamic Cranberry Vinaigrette

½ cup pure cranberry juice

2 tablespoons fructose

2 tablespoons balsamic vinegar

¼ cup onion, chopped

1 clove of garlic

½ cup olive oil

Salt and pepper to taste

Dressing Yields: 4 to 6 servings

Cut the bread into 3x1-inch sections, about 1 inch thick (each section will make one crostini) Next, drizzle just a touch of extra virgin olive oil onto each section and spread 1 large tablespoon of soy cream cheese on each. For a nice touch, top with some black and white sesame seeds. Bake them in the oven at 350° for about 8 to 10 minutes or until the bread is slightly crispy.

Meanwhile, in a blender, combine the cranberry juice with the fructose, balsamic vinegar, onion, garlic, olive oil, salt, and pepper. Blend until creamy.

Toss the greens in the vinaigrette and place mounds of dressed greens on each plate. Add a warm crostini on top of each bed of greens; and sprinkle with the basil, parsley, and toasted walnuts or pine nuts.

Roasted Vegetables with Roasted Tomato Vinaigrette

This salad is quite easily a meal. Hot-and-cold salads are a great lunch entrée because of the lack of starch and the abundance of fresh vegetables. You'll need two roasting pans for this recipe: one for vinaigrette ingredients and one for the roasted vegetables.

Ingredients Roasted Vegetables

A handful of fresh, whole mushrooms
1 large pepper (any color will do)
1 zucchini, cut in wedges
1 carrot, cut into thin wheels or thinly sliced
A few artichokes, cut in halves
Olive oil for roasting
Salt and pepper to taste

Ingredients for Tomato Vinaigrette

3 plum tomatoes, cut into halves
2 garlic cloves, sliced
¼ onion, cut into quarters
½ red bell pepper
Olive oil for roasting
Salt and pepper to taste
1 teaspoon fructose
3 tablespoons balsamic vinegar
1 bunch fresh basil (about 1 cup of leaves)
¾ cup quality olive oil for dressing
½ cup water

Yields: 4 to 6 servings

In the vinaigrette roasting pan, arrange the tomatoes, garlic, onion, and red bell pepper (flesh side up). Drizzle with olive oil (CTF) by simply rubbing each vegetable lightly with oil). Sprinkle with salt and pepper, and roast at 450° for about 20 minutes or until all vegetables have collapsed and begun to char on the edges.

In another roasting pan, arrange the mushrooms, bell pepper, zucchini, carrot, and artichokes. Drizzle them all with oil, sprinkle with salt and pepper, and roast them at the same temperature until the mushrooms are tender. You can and should pull out some vegetables before others if they stand a chance of overcooking. For instance, there is nothing worse than overcooked, mushy zucchini—take these out while they are still crisp.

To finish the vinaigrette, purée the roasted tomato ingredients with the fructose, balsamic vinegar, basil, olive oil, and water. This will work best in a food processor, but a blender will do. If the mixture seems too thick, just add a little more water to thin it. Adjust with salt and pepper and let the mixture cool in the refrigerator.

When ready to serve, toss the vegetables (chilled or warm) with your greens and the vinaigrette.

Autumn Salad with Grapes, Apples & a Walnut Vinaigrette

Autumn is such an inspiring time for me. I love to create and dedicate dishes to a season that has been so good to me. These flavors are so wonderfully spirit-warming on a brisk autumn evening. The smell of wet leaves, that first fireplace fire, and some Bach are wonderful backdrops to this dish. I like red and green seedless grapes, organic if possible, on this salad. Your apples should be firm fleshed, a red and green combination works very well too for both flavor and for visual impact.

Ingredients for Salad

Romaine lettuce, watercress, arugula &
**   frisée or your choice of greens**
Red and green grapes
Red and green apples, thinly sliced
1 red onion, thinly sliced
A few radishes, thinly sliced
2 celery stalks, thinly sliced

Ingredients for Walnut Vinaigrette

1½ tablespoons red wine vinegar
1 clove of garlic
½ cup walnuts
1 teaspoon good quality Dijon mustard
Salt and pepper to taste
3 teaspoons fructose
½ orange, juiced
½ cup olive or canola oil

Dressing Yields: 4 to 6 servings

See photo on page 61

In a food processor, combine the vinegar, garlic, walnuts, Dijon mustard, salt, pepper, fructose, and orange juice. Blend the contents while drizzling in the ½ cup of oil. Set aside

Select a mixture of greens for your base. My favorites for this salad would be a very dark green romaine, watercress, arugula, and frisée. Choose your own from your taste and from what your market has to offer—fresh is best—always. If you have your heart set on arugula, but it looks like somebody sat on it, then pass it by. You'll get it next time.

Add the sliced grapes, apples, red onion, radishes, and celery, and then arrange it! If you wish to add more touches of your own, try not to stray away from the red and green theme of this presentation —its appearance is striking.

To finish the salad, spoon the vinaigrette dressing over the entire arrangement and serve immediately with some beautiful, crusty bread...maybe some organic dairy or soy cheese—why not? And a glass of Cabernet Sauvignon, of course!

Baby Spinach Salad with Fresh Mushrooms, Vegetarian Bacon & a Horseradish Roasted Onion Vinaigrette

I don't know what it is about fresh spinach and bacon together that make it such a desirable combination. Throw in some fresh, white mushrooms and this delicious horseradish-onion dressing, and you have a classic Horizons salad that is vegan-approved and full of powerful flavors.

Ingredients for Salad

1 bag baby spinach
8 ounces fresh, white mushrooms
1 package of vegetarian bacon or ham
2 tablespoons oil (for sautéing)
Radicchio (optional)
Soy Parmesan Cheese (optional)

Ingredients for Horseradish-Onion Vinaigrette

½ large onion, quartered
3 garlic cloves
Olive oil for roasting
Salt and pepper to taste
2 tablespoons soy cream cheese
1½ to 2 tablespoon prepared horseradish
1 teaspoon quality Dijon mustard
1 teaspoon fructose
½ cup canola or olive oil
¼ cup water

Dressing Yields: 4 to 6 servings

With a roasting tray for the vinaigrette items, begin by arranging the onion with the garlic. Rub the onions and garlic with olive oil, and sprinkle with salt and pepper. Roast the onion for about 20 minutes at 450° or until it is caramelized. If you find the onion is going to burn before it cooks, then cover the roasting tray with foil.

Meanwhile, clean the spinach leaves very gently, and clean the freshest, whitest mushrooms you can find by simply brushing off any dirt. Don't wash the mushrooms unless completely necessary. Set aside.

Pour about 2 tablespoons of oil into a sauté pan and brown your favorite vegetarian bacon or ham. Remove the bacon or ham from the pan, allow it to cool on a paper towel to drain the fat, and then cut it into julienne strips. Set aside.

When the roasted onions have cooled, put them in a blender with the cream cheese, horseradish, Dijon mustard, and fructose. Blend until it has achieved a smooth and creamy consistency by slowly drizzling in the ½ cup of oil and the water.

Let the dressing cool in the refrigerator, then serve it with all the contents of the salad arranged on a plate with perhaps some croutons, some radicchio for color, and maybe a little soy parmesan cheese.

Chickpea "Tuna" Salad

Tuna salad was one of my all-time favorite foods growing up. I used to load it up with veggies and spices, and I would eat it three or four times a day. This is a fun salad to make, and chickpeas make an exceptional substitute.

Ingredients

1 (16-ounce) can of chickpeas

¼ onion, finely chopped or minced

1 celery stalk, finely chopped or minced

2 or 3 of your favorite pickles, finely chopped or minced (or 2 teaspoons relish)

Salt and pepper to taste

½ teaspoon garlic powder

1 teaspoon oregano

1 teaspoon paprika

1 teaspoon seafood seasoning or celery seed

1 teaspoon quality Dijon mustard

1 teaspoon olive oil

4 or 5 heaping tablespoons of your favorite vegan mayo (adjust to taste)

Yields: 2 to 4 servings

Drain the canned chick peas into a big bowl and mash them with a fork or potato masher until they are a rough consistency (some whole chickpeas should remain).

In another bowl, combine the onion, celery, and pickles with the salt, pepper, garlic powder, oregano, paprika, seafood seasoning (or celery seed), Dijon mustard, and olive oil. Add the vegetable and spice combination to the big bowl of crushed chick peas and mix well.

Finally, mix in the vegan mayo until it reaches your preferred consistency. I like mine right in the middle— not too dry, but not too goopy either.

Try it on wheat or rye toast with a giant tomato slice and red onion, make a hoagie, or stuff it into a tomato for a salad. Enjoy!

Seitan "Chicken" Salad

In this recipe, you can use all of your little bits and scraps of seitan—they are perfectly suited for this application. Save all of your seitan scraps in the freezer and when you are ready to use them, this is a great dish! Boiling the seitan first opens it up to receive all the flavors introduced to it in this recipe.

Ingredients for the Broth

2 quarts water
2 tablespoons seafood seasoning
2 tablespoons poultry seasoning
1 bouillon cube
    (or 1 tablespoon of broth powder)
1 pound seitan scraps

Ingredients for the Dressing

¼ onion, finely chopped or minced
1 stalk of celery, finely chopped
1 teaspoon of granulated garlic
1 teaspoon of granulated onion
1 teaspoon fructose
Salt and pepper to taste
½ teaspoon seafood seasoning
¼ teaspoon curry powder
1 drizzle of olive or canola oil
1 teaspoon quality Dijon mustard
2 teaspoons ketchup
4 to 5 heaping tablespoons of your favorite
    vegan mayo (adjust to taste)

Yields: 2 to 4 servings

See photo on page 62

Boil your water with the seafood seasoning, poultry seasoning, and bouillon cube. Add the seitan scraps and return to a boil. Boil for about 3 minutes. Remove the pot from the heat, drain the seitan, and let it cool. Draining it and cooling it adequately are extremely important! Shake the seitan around in a colander and press on it a bit with paper towels. Any remaining water will make the salad less creamy. Once it is dry, chill it for at least an hour.

Then, in a large mixing bowl, combine the onion, celery, granulated garlic, granulated onion, fructose, salt, pepper, seafood seasoning, and curry powder. Add the dried, cooled seitan scraps to this mixture, and mix in the Dijon mustard, ketchup, and vegan mayo.

Serve this salad chilled on toasted, whole wheat bread; in a pita; or on a bed of greens. It makes a great hors d'oeuvre for parties or football games!

Hearts of Palm, Mango & Avocado Salad

Hearts of palm are such an icon of exotic food for me. We were fortunate enough to find them fresh recently on the big island of Hawaii. We were served a delicious salad, where they were marinated in a lemongrass vinaigrette. This recipe is for more of a relish that goes great with Jamaican grilled-and-chilled tofu, but it could easily be a main course for lunch over mixed greens with some plantain chips and roasted macadamia nuts. You'll love the way sliced hearts of palm shred and take on the appearance of crab when tossed.

Ingredients

½ Hass avocado, just ripened; finely diced
    or roughly mashed
1 plastic-lined can or jar of unmarinated
    hearts of palm, thinly sliced or run through
    the slicer blade of a food processor
¼ cup vegan mayo
1 teaspoon quality Dijon mustard
Drizzle of extra virgin olive oil
1 lime, juiced
½ mango, finely diced
½ red bell pepper, diced
¼ cup onion, minced
Salt and pepper to taste
1 teaspoon fructose

Yields: 2 to 4 servings

See photo on page 129

Toss all of the ingredients gently together and:

- Serve over grilled pineapple spears as an appetizer,
- Use as a relish for grilled or pan-seared tofu, or
- Stuff into a tomato for a summer lunch.

Cabbage & Cilantro Salad

Cabbage is the main ingredient on most salads on mainland Belize. At my hotel, a jungle lodge near the Guatemalan border, I had one of my favorite salads ever. It was cabbage and cilantro, which came right from the hotel's organic garden, tossed in a subtle vinaigrette .

Ingredients

½ head of white cabbage, shredded
1 bunch cilantro, leaves picked off
¼ cup olive oil
2 teaspoons quality Dijon mustard
1 lemon, juiced
¼ teaspoon salt
¼ teaspoon pepper
¼ teaspoon fructose

Yields: 2 servings

Place the cabbage and cilantro in a large bowl and set aside.

In a small bowl, combine the oil, Dijon mustard, lemon juice, salt, pepper, and fructose and stir to mix thoroughly.

Next, pour the mixture over the cabbage and cilantro and toss lightly. Let salad sit for a few minutes so the cabbage absorbs the dressing.

Red & Yellow Tomato Salad with Charred Fennel

This "right of summer" doesn't get any better! If you don't have fresh-garden tomatoes, buy local organic tomatoes, and your results will be superb. Here's the trick to any good tomato salad: salt your tomatoes. It tenderizes them and makes them release their water, which then becomes part of the vinaigrette.

Ingredients:

1 red tomato; sliced, diced or wedged

1 yellow tomato (preferably in season and ripe), sliced, diced or wedged

A few dashes of salt

1 small bulb of fennel (you won't use it all)

Pepper to taste

2 teaspoons extra virgin olive oil

Fresh basil leaves

Splash of balsamic vinegar (optional)

Yields: 2 servings

See photo on page 60

Slice the tomatoes into wheels as thick as you like. They may also be diced or cut into wedges. Lightly salt each piece and set aside.

Meanwhile, peel off a section of fennel, preferably more towards the inside, and rub it with just a bit of oil to coat it. Then, carefully using tongs, hold it directly over the flame of a gas-stove burner to char the edges. If you have an electric range, then put the fennel on a tray under the broiler at as high a temperature as you can for about 3 to 4 minutes. When charred, cut the fennel into little thin strips and sprinkle them on the tomatoes, along with the olive oil, pepper, basil leaves, and balsamic vinegar.

Asian Vegetable Slaw with Grapefruit Sesame Vinaigrette

This is a great, light salad for an outdoor lunch in spring, when the mornings and nights are too cold but the daytime temperature has your heart singing. I love the way this salad has arranged sections of shredded vegetables, allowing you to pick or mix them while you eat. Its a wonderful expression of color and freshness, and the Asian-influenced vinaigrette adds just the right amount of flavor without masking the natural goodness of the fresh vegetables.

Ingredients for Slaw

1 daikon, shredded
2 carrots, peeled and shredded
¼ head of red or green cabbage, shredded
2 scallions, chopped
Sprouts (your choice)
Lettuce (your choice)

Ingredients for Grapefruit Sesame Vinaigrette

½ grapefruit, juiced
⅓ cup toasted sesame oil
2 tablespoon rice wine vinegar
2 tablespoon soy sauce
2 teaspoon freshly grated ginger
1 smashed garlic clove
1 tablespoon fructose (adjust according to your
   desired grapefruit tartness or sweetness)
¼ cup canola oil
Dash salt
Black or white pepper to taste
¼ cup scallions, chopped
1 teaspoon quality Dijon mustard
1 teaspoon wasabi or Chinese mustard
   (optional)
¼ cup water

Yields: 2 to 4 servings

Arrange the shredded vegetables in different sections over a bed of greens and set aside.

In a salad shaker, food processor, or small bowl, combine the dressing ingredients and mix well. This is a loose vinaigrette.

Just before serving, shake or mix the vinaigrette once more and drizzle over the greens and vegetables.

Curried Cucumber Rice Salad

My mom used to make this salad for parties when we were young. I was always intrigued by the exotic taste of the curry. Now I make my own version for parties. Sautéing the curry first in oil is the secret to bringing out all of its wonderful fragrance.

Ingredients

3 cups precooked jasmine or basmati rice
(or your favorite type)
1 tablespoon curry powder
3 tablespoons olive or canola oil
1 cucumber, chopped
1 tomato, chopped
1 small onion, chopped
½ teaspoon toasted sesame oil
1 teaspoon fructose
1 teaspoon mustard
¼ cup vegan mayo
Juice of a lemon
Salt and pepper to taste

Yields: 4 to 6 servings

See photo on page 129

Place the precooked rice in a large mixing bowl and set aside. Sauté the curry power in the olive oil for about 1 to 2 minutes to bring out the fragrance. Don't let it burn. Then, let it cool.

Add the curry mixture, as well as the remaining ingredients, to the rice bowl and stir in thoroughly. Chill the salad in the refrigerator for at least 20 minutes before serving.

Irish Seitan Beef Stew (page 36)

Foreground: Cajun Lentil Soup with Vegetarian Sausage (page 26); background: U T Cornbread (page 147)

Top Left: Creamy Carrot Soup (page 27)

Top Right: Roasted Vegetable Gazpacho with Avocado Aioli (page 25)

Bottom: Drunken Caribbean Black Bean Soup with Vegan Mango Crema (page 34)

*Top Left: Tortilla Soup
with Roasted Seitan
(Sopa de Tortilla)
(page 33)*

*Bottom Left: Red &
Yellow Tomato Salad
with Charred Fennel
(page 54)*

*Right: Autumn Salad
with Grapes, Apples &
a Walnut Vinaigrette
(page 48)*

Hearts of Palm, Jicama & Orange Salad with Lemon Cilantro Vinaigrette (page 44)

Seitan "Chicken" Salad (page 51)

Avocado, White Bean & Smoked Tofu Salad with Agave Mustard Vinaigrette (page 45)

The Honduran Rainforest

. . . .

*Not far from La Ceiba in Northern Honduras is a remarkable place
called Pico Bonito. I have dedicated many a dish at the restaurant to
this truly inspiring place...*

*Outside of our comfortable cabin is an enormous avocado tree
that drops its fruit with a loud thump on the deck in the middle of the
night. Over coffee the next morning, I gaze up at this incredible tree,
avocados just dangling everywhere. I laugh at the vision of myself
carrying in a big box of avocados to the restaurant for which I pay a
small fortune. Behind the deck is a cocoa tree, and down the path to
the butterfly farm are rows and rows of lime, orange, and mango
trees. This is where the chef of Pico Bonito comes to get produce.*

*As we set out for our hike that day, I take note of the waterfalls
that you can see trickling down the distant mountains. No, we aren't
going that far up, but as we pass through the tropical gardens of the
lodge to the trails, my mind overrun with fresh cooking ideas, I grin in
content: This is the perfect place!*

*We hike for a while up into the spectacular rainforest. The flowers
and plants are of unimaginable shapes and colors; the trees are of a
cartoon fairytale. It rains, and then it rains hard. We don't turn back
because we are in the rainforest after all—what did we expect?*

The views we took in that day will stay with us forever. It was that intense. Watching the dense clouds roll over and down the mountains was so powerful. The air was so fresh and clean, and there were times that we could not have been convinced what century we were in. We head back to the hotel, soaking wet. Our clothes soaked up the rain, but our spirits soaked up feelings we will carry for at least a lifetime.

Back at the hotel grounds, the waterfalls on the distant mountain are now huge; you can hear them thunder in the distance.

"How long is that hike?" I ask the hotel manager. "A day, señor." he says.

A good reason to go back. It's always nice to be happy with what you are doing in life, but how pleasant it is to know there is still more to do.

That evening, we sip our cocktails on the porch of the lodge. The waterfalls are back to a distant trickle. We are still half speechless from our moving experience of the day. As I sip my rum and sour orange, I think, "This would make a great sauce!"

RSL
Pico Bonito, La Ceiba, Honduras
29 May 2002

Appetizers

· ·

In order for people to first get interested in meatless cuisine, their first taste needs to be a winner. A great way to introduce people to new foods and flavors is through small appetizer-sized portions, either at a family dinner or a party. Here are a few variations of some classic appetizers and some unique Horizons favorites that will ease people into some new ingredients in a comfortable and very tasty way!

Kate plates a hot, smoked tofu & wild mushroom enchilada, right out the oven. This Horizons appetizer has been on the dinner menu for years, and many of its flavors can be found in the cookbook recipes as well.

Caribbean Seitan BBQ Wings

I did a live-TV demonstration of these wings on CN8's "Your Morning." I was scared crazy, but somehow managed to talk and cook my way through it. This recipe is a home-friendly version of Horizon's most popular appetizer. More than anything else, they have made believers of many skeptics. The secret here is a very thin pan, making for very little distance between your fire and your seitan.

Ingredients for BBQ Sauce

¼ cup ketchup

1 teaspoon molasses

2 tablespoon agave syrup

¼ lime, juiced

1 teaspoon ginger juice (grate fresh ginger and squeeze)

2 teaspoon jerk or Cajun spice (use a brand that contains salt or make your own using the recipe in the *Getting Started* section)

Ingredients for Seitan

2 tablespoon olive or canola oil

10 to 12 ounces of seitan; drained, rinsed, and patted dry

Yields: 2 servings

Mix all the BBQ sauce ingredients in a mixing bowl. Set aside.

Break up seitan into wing-sized portions. Heat a wok or thin frying pan on high heat and then add the oil. When the oil starts to ripple (almost smoking), gently add the seitan by sliding it down the sides of the pan one at a time. Brown the seitan "wings" on each side, turning them with tongs.

When browned, add the BBQ sauce to the seitan and let it caramelize around the seitan. When the sauce has stuck to the seitan and turned a dark crimson color, they're done. The sauce process should take no more than 1 minute. Don't overcook or the sauce will burn. Remove from heat and serve immediately.

Note: Leftover BBQ sauce will keep for up to 7 to 10 days in the refrigerator.

Variation: For a zesty *Chipotle Seitan BBQ Wing*, add 1 to 2 chipotles, either canned or dried (rehydrated with some warm water), 1 teaspoon Dijon mustard, and the juice of a whole lime (rather than a ¼ lime) to the BBQ sauce ingredients shown above. Mix in a blender until smooth.

Seitan Skewers with Curry BBQ Sauce

Curry is not just for Indian and Thai food. It's a fragrant, uplifting spice. In this sauce, you'll be surprised at how curry can complement BBQ.

Ingredients for BBQ Sauce

¼ cup onion, chopped
2 teaspoon garlic, crushed
1 teaspoon ginger, freshly grated
2 tablespoons oil
2 teaspoon curry powder
¼ cup rum or water
2 tablespoon tamari soy sauce
½ cup ketchup
1 teaspoon molasses
2 tablespoon fructose

Ingredients for Seitan

20 ounces of seitan chunks, drained, rinsed,
    and patted dry
2 tablespoons olive or canola oil
Salt and pepper to taste

Yields: 2 to 4 servings

See photo on page 103

Preheat your grill to medium-high. If using wooden skewers, soak them first for about 30 minutes.

Then, sauté the onion, garlic, and ginger in the oil until lightly browned. Add the curry and cook 1 minute longer. Deglaze with the rum and let the liquid reduce slightly (about 1 minute).

Next, in a blender combine the sautéed mixture with the soy sauce, ketchup, molasses and fructose. Blend until smooth. Set aside.

Skewer the seitan. Rub on the oil, salt, and pepper, and grill the skewers on high heat, letting the seitan lightly char on all sides.

Remove the seitan skewers and cover the seitan in the BBQ sauce. When ready to serve, finish them in a hot oven (450°) for 7 to 8 minutes. Or, if you prefer, you can return them to the grill on low heat to avoid the sauce from burning.

Jamaican Mango Jerk Seitan Tips

On the island of Jamaica, visitors are introduced to a unique concept called "jerk." I discovered the real thing at some food huts tucked under palm trees on Negril Beach, which is on the west coast of this majestic, mountainous island. With aspects of BBQ, Cajun and African spice, jerk is either wet or dry, but will always contain thyme, allspice and some kind of heat. There are as many jerk recipes as there are cooks, and although this "from-scratch" recipe is time consuming, I think it's worth it.

Ingredients

½ cup onion, chopped
1 teaspoon garlic, chopped
1 tablespoon ginger, chopped
4 tablespoons canola or olive oil
1 teaspoon dried thyme
1 teaspoon ground cumin
1 teaspoon allspice
1 teaspoon paprika
¼ cup soy sauce
¼ cup bell or chile pepper, chopped
1 cup vegetable broth or water
2 tablespoons agave or fructose
2 tablespoons ketchup
½ ripe mango, peeled and chopped
1 teaspoon molasses
12 ounces seitan, cut into bite-sized pieces

Yields: 2 servings, plus extra sauce

Sauté the onion, garlic, and ginger in the 2 tablespoons of oil for 5 minutes. Add the dry spices and sauté for 1 more minute. Then, add the rest of the ingredients, except the seitan. Simmer for 5 more minutes. Place the mixture in a blender and purée until smooth. Set aide.

To cook the seitan use a hot wok with the 2 tablespoon of oil . When the oil starts to ripple (almost smoking), gently slide the seitan down the sides of the pan. Let the seitan get as crispy as possible on both sides.

Pour ½ cup of the jerk sauce over the seitan and let it caramelize around the seitan. When it all sticks to the seitan and the pan is dry, the seitan tips are done. Serve immediately.

Stuffed Artichoke Bottoms New Orleans

New Orleans is one of those wild culinary experiences. This is a serious eatin' town. Spicy Cajun and elegant Creole food abound, restaurants everywhere. The smells, the sound of Dixie, the feel of the Deep South—welcome to the Bayou! While there, I ate at a restaurant called the Pelican Club and had a stuffed artichoke bottom appetizer. Here's a cleaned-up, Horizonized version of a classic Creole offering.

Artichoke Preparation

24 ounces of artichoke bottoms
    (fresh or canned)
A drizzle of olive oil
Cracked black pepper to taste

Ingredients for Stuffing

1 large tomato, finely chopped
½ medium onion, finely chopped
1 green bell pepper, finely chopped
8 ounces vegetarian sausage
    (cooked lightly and then finely chopped)
2 tablespoons garlic, minced
1½ tablespoon Creole or Cajun Spice blend
    (see the *Getting Started* section)
1 teaspoon olive oil
1 teaspoon quality Dijon mustard
¼ cup bread crumbs

Yields: 4 servings

See photo on page 101

Unless you really want to go to the trouble of cleansing and preparing fresh artichokes, I suggest you seek out the canned or jarred variety. To refresh the canned or jarred artichokes, boil them in salted water for about 4 minutes. Then strain the artichokes and put them in a bowl. Add a drizzle of olive oil and some cracked black pepper.

For the stuffing, finely chop the tomato and pass the liquid through a strainer. Then, add the onion, green bell pepper, vegetarian sausage, and garlic to the tomato. Add the Creole or Cajun spice blend.

Next, drizzle 1 tablespoon of olive oil over the mixture (CTF by using stock instead of oil) and the Dijon mustard. Fold in the bread crumbs.

Stuff the artichoke bottoms with this mixture and bake them in an ovenware dish for about 12 minutes at 450°.

Smoked Tofu Island Cocktail

I love cocktail sauce, and I love it even more when it's spiked with island flavors. This is an easy appetizer if you just want to buy some prepackaged smoked or baked tofu.

Ingredients

8 to 16 ounces smoked tofu
1 cup ketchup
⅔ cup prepared horseradish
1 lime, juiced
½ teaspoon allspice
1 teaspoon fresh thyme
½ orange, juiced
1 tablespoon fructose

Yields: 2 to 4 servings

See photo on page 102

If you have a smoker, by all means, smoke your own tofu; otherwise, use your favorite store-bought brand. You can cut the smoked tofu into cubes, strips, triangles, or more interesting shapes, such as scallops or even carve out shrimp!

For the cocktail sauce, mix the ketchup and horseradish. Add the lime juice, allspice, thyme, orange juice, and fructose. Mix well, and you're ready to go.

Vegetarian Clams Casino

Textured soy protein (TSP) granules work very well as a clam substitute. Chop the vegetables as finely as you can, and you'll get some wonderful results from this Horizonized 70's classic. For baking, use small gratin dishes or foil tart pans. Make a pot of our Vegetarian Manhattan Clam Chowder, some corn, potato salad, and watermelon, and you've got an incredible, animal-free, seashore lunch or dinner.

Ingredients

1 quart water

1 tablespoon and 1 teaspoon of seafood
    seasoning

1 tablespoon granulated garlic

1 cup TSP granules (chunks will not work)

½ onion, minced

1 green bell pepper, minced

3 cloves garlic, minced

½ cup vegetarian bacon, chopped
    very fine (optional)

2 tablespoons olive or canola oil

2 tablespoons soy margarine

2 tablespoon dried oregano

Salt and pepper to taste

¼ cup fresh parsley

¼ cup white wine

1 lemon, juiced

¼ cup bread crumbs (optional)

Yields: 8 to 10 servings

Boil the water. Add 1 tablespoon of the seafood seasoning and the granulated garlic. Add the TSP granules, and bring to a boil for about 4 or 5 minutes. Drain the water and set the TSP granules aside.

Meanwhile, sauté the onion, bell pepper, garlic, and vegetarian bacon (if you choose to use it) in oil (CTF by sautéing in broth instead). Add the soy margarine (again, CTF by using broth). Season with 1 teaspoon of seafood seasoning as well as the oregano, parsley, salt, and pepper. Stir in the white wine and lemon juice. Add the TSP to the vegetable mixture and stir.

Once some of the liquid has been absorbed and the mixture has blended well, transfer it to your chosen baking dishes and bake for about 10 minutes at 400°. If you wish, the optional bread crumbs sprinkled on top will make an excellent crust.

Stuffed Portabella Mushroom with Spinach & Tofu Ricotta

Portabella mushrooms have become quite popular in restaurants lately. A great vegetarian option, they are meaty and satisfying. Here we have a preparation that involves blanching the mushrooms to tenderize them, or you can grill them if you want extra flavor.

Ingredients for Marinade

2 teaspoons and ½ cup olive oil for the
    vinaigrette
1 splash of balsamic vinegar
1 splash tamari soy sauce
1 teaspoon ground black pepper

Ingredients for Mushrooms & Stuffing

1 quart of water
2 portabella mushrooms
1 bowl ice water
16 ounces fresh spinach, washed and trimmed
¼ pound tofu, crumbled
1 tablespoon olive oil
Salt and pepper to taste
1 teaspoon good quality Dijon mustard
1 teaspoon garlic, minced
¼ cup fresh basil, chopped
2 teaspoons walnuts or pine nuts, crushed
1 plum tomato, minced

Yields: 2 servings

In a mixing bowl, make your marinade of 2 teaspoons of olive oil and the balsamic vinegar, tamari, and ground black pepper. Set aside.

Bring a medium pot of water to a boil. Drop the mushrooms into the boiling water for 2 minutes, then remove them, and put them into the marinade bowl.

Fill another bowl with ice water. Drop the spinach into the same water in which you just blanched the mushrooms. Just when the leaves start to wilt and the color turns bright green, drain the spinach from the water (or save the water for a stock base) and transfer it immediately into the ice water to stop the cooking process. When cooled, drain the spinach and squeeze out all of the excess water. Set aside.

In yet another mixing bowl, crumble the tofu and drizzle in 1 tablespoon of olive oil as well as the salt and pepper, Dijon mustard, minced garlic, basil, and crushed walnuts or pine nuts. Add the spinach and toss lightly.

Place the portabella mushrooms on a baking sheet (topside down) and fill them with the tofu mixture. Bake at 450° for about 10 minutes. Save the resulting mushroom marinade for the sauce!

Finely chop the plum tomato and drain out all the water from it. Sprinkle a little salt on it. When you remove the mushrooms from the oven, top each with a mound of chopped tomato.

Put the mushroom marinade into a blender (include the mushroom marinade from baking), and blend it while drizzling in enough oil (about ½ cup) so that it emulsifies. Before serving, surround each mushroom with a little pool of this vinaigrette.

Atlantic Tofu Gratin

Here's another seashore-inspired recipe. This one is a luscious baked, bubbly gratin of tofu "seafood." Don't let the long list of ingredients deter you. It's relatively easy to make. To make it work best, the tofu must be pre-baked.

Ingredients for Tofu Marinade

¹/₃ cup olive oil
1 small green bell pepper, chopped
1 small onion, chopped
1 teaspoon garlic, chopped
1 tablespoon seafood seasoning
1 small tomato, chopped
1 lemon, juiced
1 pinch curry powder
1 teaspoon dried thyme
1 teaspoon quality Dijon mustard
2 teaspoons white wine or sherry
½ pound tofu, chopped

Ingredients for Dressing

2 tablespoons olive oil
2 tablespoons quality Dijon mustard
1 tablespoon vegan mayo
½ teaspoon fructose or sugar
¹/₃ cup vegetable stock or water

Optional Ingredients

4 pieces veggie bacon, cooked and crumbled
16 ounces spinach, washed and dried
½ cup soy cheese, shredded

Yields: 4 servings

See photo on page 104

Combine all *Tofu Marinade* ingredients and bake on a sheet pan at 450° for 20 minutes, turning the tofu with a spoon twice. Then place the mixture in a gratin dish. You may add some veggie bacon or spinach if you like.

Next, combine the *Dressing* ingredients in a blender and mix until smooth. Cover the tofu mixture with it, and top with cheese if you like.

Bake on highest oven setting (500°) for about 10 minutes or until the top is brown and bubbly. You may finish the gratin under the broiler for last-minute color.

Costa Rican Breakfast Quesadilla

Costa Rica is a most beautiful country with its lush rainforest, soaring mountains, and warm tropical waters! Outside of Quepos, on the road to Manuel Antonio National Park, are many funky hotels and lodges with open verandas on which to have a meal surrounded by lush jungle. Breakfast is Tico style with scrambled eggs; black beans; rice; and warm, soft tortillas. This quesadilla is my tribute to this spectacular land.

Ingredients

6 ounces black beans
½ teaspoon olive oil and 2 tablespoons (for cooking the tofu)
2 tablespoons tomato, chopped
A few dashes of hot sauce
½ bunch fresh cilantro (leaves only), chopped
1 teaspoon fructose
¼ teaspoon salt
½ teaspoon pepper
¼ teaspoon island spice (see *Getting Started*)
1 tablespoon onion, minced
1 lime (for garnish)
4 ounces tofu, crumbled
¼ cup cheese of your choice
1 tortilla (large burrito size)
Salsa and condiments of your choice

Yields: 1 to 2 servings

Lightly mash the black beans with a fork, and then dress them with the ½ teaspoon olive oil, tomato, hot sauce (to your liking), cilantro, and fructose. Add the salt, pepper, and island spice.

Using 2 tablespoons of olive oil, cook the crumbled tofu with the mined onion in a nonstick pan for about 5 minutes over medium heat. Set aside.

Spread the bean mixture onto half of a side of tortilla, and put the crumbled tofu mix on top. (This recipe makes one tortilla.) On the other half, put your favorite soy cheese (smoked cheese works very well).

Bake the tortilla, open-faced, in a 450° oven for about 7 minutes or until the cheese melts and the edges of the tortilla are crisp.

Remove the tortilla from the oven and fold it in half so that the cheese covers the bean mixture. Cut the tortilla into 3 or 4 wedges. Serve with your favorite salsa and condiments, such as soy sour cream, guacamole, and jalapenos.

Tuscan White Bean Dip with Olives

It's a shame that when some people think of Italian food, they tend to think only of spaghetti marinara and parmigiana. Italian cuisine is so full of fresh, wonderful flavors: fruity, rich olive oils; plump white beans; and the most beautiful lemons that you've ever seen. Here's a dish that features some wonderful Italian flavors. A hummus from across the Mediterranean.

Ingredients

**32 ounces cannellini beans, canned
    (or any white bean)**
½ cup extra virgin olive oil
6 ounces green olives, pitted
3 ounces black olives, pitted
**1 roasted red pepper
    (jarred red peppers work just fine)**
Salt and pepper to taste
1 dash cumin
1 teaspoon paprika
½ cup fresh basil
2 garlic cloves
¼ onion, chopped
1 lemon, juiced

Yields: 6 to 8 servings

Combine all ingredients in a food processor and purée until smooth. Drizzle in some water if you find it necessary to thin the dip.

Serve with warm Italian bread, crackers, or crudités.

Cuban Nachos

One day, while connecting flights in Miami airport on our way to Roatan, we had a snack at a tropical café and ordered plantain chip nachos. We were served a giant plate of stale, broken chips with something resembling cheese whiz and sour cream. As we tried to eat them, I said, "You know, there's potential here. We could do this." And, we did...our Cuban Nachos have been on the menu ever since. I found a company called Inka Crops, where all they do is distribute roasted plantain chips (Inka Chips™) from Peru. This isn't so much a recipe for you, but an idea. Go with it where you want. You can use our guacamole and salsa recipes or buy them to make it easy.

Ingredients

16 ounces plantain chips
Black beans, drained and rinsed
 (refried beans work well too)
Soy cheese, shredded
1 dollop soy or dairy sour cream (optional)
1 dollop guacamole (optional)
1 heaping tablespoon salsa (optional)
1 tablespoon fresh mango, chopped (optional)
1 scallion, finely chopped (optional)

Yields: 2 to 4 servings

See photo on page 103

Layer the chips, beans and cheese in an ovenware dish and bake it at 400° for about 10 minutes or until the cheese melts. Then, garnish with your choice of toppings. At the restaurant, we also add fresh mango, which I think pairs perfectly with black beans.

Gratin of Mushrooms & Artichokes

Ah, the comfort of gratin. The ingredients are put into an ovenware dish and baked with a golden bubbly cheese top—delicious! Jarred artichokes are preferable to canned, but always buy UN-marinated. Never let others decide your spices for you. Fresh is always best, of course, but fresh artichokes require a lot of prep. In our version, we'll go with both soy cheese and sauce, but don't worry, it's still as decadent as you would hope.

Ingredients

2 quarts water
1 pound fresh white mushrooms
8 to 10 whole artichokes, quartered
1 teaspoon quality Dijon mustard
2 tablespoons olive oil
Salt and pepper to taste
1 teaspoon fresh rosemary
1 teaspoon fresh thyme
1 teaspoon fresh basil
8 ounces soy cream cheese
¼ cup white wine
½ cup stock
2 cloves garlic
1 tablespoon extra virgin olive oil
½ cup soy mozzarella cheese
¼ cup soy parmesan cheese

Yields: 2 to 4 servings

While the water comes to a boil, slice the mushrooms in halves and add them to the boiling water, along with the artichoke quarters. Once the water returns to a boil, allow it to boil for about 3 minutes, which will tenderize the artichokes and blanch the mushrooms. Remove the vegetables from the water and place them in a bowl with the Dijon mustard, olive oil, salt, pepper, rosemary, thyme, and basil.

In a blender, combine the soy cream cheese with the white wine, stock, garlic cloves, and olive oil. Puree until smooth, and then add to the mushroom and artichoke mixture.

Transfer the mushroom and artichoke mixture into one large baking gratin or into several smaller, individual gratin dishes and cover them with the soy mozzarella and soy parmesan. Unfortunately, fat-free cheese will not work very well in this application. Bake until bubbly (about 15 minutes at 450°), and then serve hot with crusty French bread.

Roasted Peppers with Caramelized Onions, Olives & Capers

Fresh, roasted peppers are a thing of beauty. Canned and jarred are okay for sauces, salsa, and seasoning, but to enjoy roasted peppers to their fullest intensity, you should roast them from fresh, beautiful peppers. Enjoy these peppers with some nice Italian or French bread.

Ingredients

6 red and yellow peppers
A drizzle of olive oil and $1/3$ **cup**
Salt and pepper to taste
1 tablespoon garlic, minced
2 medium onions
1 tablespoon balsamic vinegar
Capers
Exotic black olives
2 tablespoons fresh parsley (or basil)

Yields: 2 to 4 servings

See photo on page 104

Set your oven to 500° and put the peppers on a baking sheet. Roast them for about 10 minutes, and then turn them over, one by one. Cook the peppers until they are relatively soft on all sides. Remove the peppers from the oven and cover them with foil or place them in a plastic container with a lid. Let them stand until they are cool enough to touch, and then peel the skins. Save some of the juice from the peppers and pass it through a strainer to remove the seeds. To finish the peppers, add the strained liquid, a drizzle of olive oil, salt, pepper, and some the minced garlic. Set aside.

Meanwhile, slice your onions very thin. Lay the onions flat on another baking sheet and drizzle them with olive oil, balsamic vinegar, salt, and pepper. Roast them until they are completely glazed and sticky. This should take about 30 minutes at 400°.

For presentation, I like to lay out the peppers and spread the onions on top. Place the olives all around the plate, and do the same with the capers. Top the whole dish with the parsley or basil to bring it all together.

Sides, Salsas, Relishes & Dips

. . . .

In this section, we have a selection of different rices, potatoes, vegetables, dipping sauces and toppings for you to explore. Some have been suggested as accompaniments to other dishes in this cookbook, and many are good just on their own. Even though this chapter is about sides, there is a lot of technique here that is the foundation of good cooking.

Working side by side, Rich and Kate put together another fabulous entrée. Presentation is key at Horizons—the gateway to delicious, gourmet meatless cuisine.

Black Bean & Rice Griddle Cakes

Here's a simple preparation with restaurant-style results. Use these griddle cakes as a pedestal for a pan-seared tofu recipe. They also work well with white beans for a Mediterranean-style dish.

Ingredients

2 cups white rice, cooked

1 (15-ounce) can of black beans, drained and rinsed

2 ounces coconut milk

1 teaspoon Tropical Spice blend (see the *Getting Started* section)

1 teaspoon vegetable or canola oil for each cake

Yields: 4 servings

See photo on page 101

Roughly purée the black beans in a food processor with the coconut milk. Add the spice blend, and then fold the bean purée into the rice with your hands.

Pressing firmly, form the mixture into cakes about 1 inch thick. Cook each cake on a griddle or in nonstick pan with 1 teaspoon of oil (for each cake) and brown both sides.

<u>Note</u>: You'll need a starchy rice for this recipe, so be sure to use sushi rice, jasmine, or Chinese sticky rice. Don't rinse the rice before cooking.

Braised White Beans

The effect of foil-roasting beans is incredible. They will come out soft, silky, full of deep flavor, and even a little cheesy. We suggest that you team this heartwarming side with the Roasted Portabella Mushroom entree (refer to page 111 for the recipe).

Ingredients

2 (12 to 16 ounce) can of navy, great northern, or white kidney beans; drained and rinsed

2 garlic cloves, crushed

1 sprig rosemary

1 sprig thyme

1 sprig tarragon

1 sprig oregano

1 tablespoon white wine or Madeira wine

2 tablespoons extra virgin olive oil

¼ cup mushroom stock (if you have extra from your mushrooms) or vegetable broth

1 dash black pepper, coarsely ground

Yields: 4 servings

Preheat your oven to 400º. Mix all ingredients and bake in a casserole or oven sheet pan covered with a lid or foil for 20 to 25 minutes. Carefully uncover and remove the herb sprigs. Stir and serve.

Grilled Vegetable Ratatouille

Ratatouille—you just never see this stuff anymore. Maybe it's because of the mushy zucchini and canned tomato slosh that we've had our bad experiences with that this dish has become so outcast. But ratatouille, when done right, is exquisite. Here we lighten it up by using fresh tomatoes and by grilling the zucchini just to al dente *to keep everything crisp and fresh.*

Ingredients

2 medium zucchini
Olive oil (enough to brush the vegetables)
Balsamic vinegar (enough to brush the vegetables)
Salt and pepper to taste
1 onion
6 tomatoes
1 red bell pepper
2 tablespoons extra virgin olive oil
½ lemon, juiced
½ cup fresh basil, chopped
2 tablespoons fresh thyme

Yields: 4 servings

Cut the zucchini lengthwise into quarters, and brush them with olive oil and balsamic vinegar and sprinkle them with salt and pepper.

On a char grill on high heat, cook the zucchini on each side until you see nice grill marks. Don't overcook it! If the top starts to really sweat, flip them immediately. Overcooked zucchini, in my view, is completely unpalatable.

Next, cut your onion into 4 big rings and brush it with the same oil, vinegar, salt, and pepper. You want to grill the onion really well.

Meanwhile, cut your tomatoes in half and brush them with the same marinade. Then, grill them on one side only (flesh/flat side down) until you have nice grill marks. Cut the bell pepper into thick rings or lengthwise into 3 to 4 "flaps." Use the same grilling process.

Chop all of these vegetables to about ½ dice. In a large bowl, toss the vegetables with the extra virgin olive oil, lemon juice, basil, and thyme. There should be enough salt and pepper in the marinade to season the dish, but add more if desired.

Escarole with White Beans

Here's a nice, light adaptation of an Italian classic. One of my favorite vegetables is escarole. It's so full of flavor that it will make its own aromatic broth. The texture is fresh and slightly chewy—a very satisfying and colorful green vegetable. I like great northern beans, but if you want to go for authenticity, use cannellini beans, which are also known as white kidney beans.

Ingredients

1 head escarole
1 (15-ounce) can of white beans
2 tablespoons olive oil
1 tablespoon garlic, crushed
¼ cup white wine
½ cup stock
Salt and pepper to taste
Extra virgin olive oil (to drizzle over dish)

Yields: 2 to 4 servings

Clean the escarole and roughly chop. Rinse and drain the white beans. Set both items aside.

Heat the olive oil in a large skillet. Add the crushed garlic and have your white wine in hand and ready to go. When the garlic starts to brown a bit, remove the skillet from the heat and add the white wine. Return the skillet to the heat and bring to a boil. Allow to reduce by a least half.

Add the stock and the escarole. Let it adjust to the heat for about 45 seconds, and then start turning it with tongs. Once the escarole starts to wilt (we're working faster here!), add salt, pepper, and the beans.

When the escarole no longer looks raw (when it just begins to look cooked and wilted), it is done. Don't overcook the greens! Make sure to save the broth.

Finish it with a drizzle of extra virgin olive oil and serve with fresh Italian bread and a spoon so that your diners may enjoy every flavorful bit.

Spinach with Garlic & Pine Nuts

Don't ever shortchange yourself on spinach. Buy the best you can. The pre-washed, pre-trimmed, bagged spinach will make you love to work with it. Buy dirty and stemmy spinach, and you'll hate it.

Ingredients

2 tablespoons quality olive oil

½ cup stock (or water)

2 teaspoons garlic

2 tablespoons pine nuts

1 pound spinach, cleaned

Salt and pepper to taste

2 tablespoons lemon juice (optional)

2 tablespoons extra virgin olive oil (optional)

2 tablespoons soy parmesan (optional)

Yields: 2 to 4 servings

Heat the olive oil in a large skillet on medium heat. Have your stock on hand. Put the garlic in the oil and stir with a wooden spoon. Add the pine nuts. When the garlic starts to brown, add the stock. Place the spinach on top of the heated garlic and pine nuts and turn it with tongs. Add salt and pepper to taste.

Cook until the spinach has wilted completely, but while it is still bright green. It's important to let the spinach cook evenly, and it's crucial to pull it out at the right time. Remember that the spinach will cook a little more once you've removed it from the skillet. You have a window of only seconds before it overcooks. The pressure's on!

If there is juice left in the pan, make sure you serve it with the greens. For a last-minute garnish, try fresh lemon and extra virgin olive oil or maybe a little soy parmesan.

Baby Carrots with Horseradish & Curry

This dish works so well since horseradish and curry, when used with restraint, are wonderful compliments to each other. The bright, orange color and the sweetness of the carrots just emphasize this dynamic.

Ingredients

1 pound baby carrots

½ cup stock

1 teaspoon quality curry powder

1 teaspoon garlic, minced

1 tablespoon prepared horseradish

2 teaspoons fructose

1 teaspoon salt

2 tablespoons fresh parsley, chopped

1 teaspoon paprika

1 tablespoon soy cream cheese or olive oil

Yields: 4 servings

Boil the baby carrots in lightly salted water for about 8 minutes or until they are just tender, but not at all mushy!

In a saucepan, heat the stock with the curry powder, garlic, horseradish, fructose, salt, and cream cheese or olive oil (or CTF by not adding any cream cheese or olive oil).

When the carrots are done, simply drain them and add them to the sauce. Cook the carrots in the sauce for about a minute to meld the flavors. Sprinkle with fresh parsley and paprika to serve.

Mushrooms with Five Onion Confit

A confit is an age-old, French technique. By adding some oil to the onions and roasting them, we will caramelize them, bringing out their natural sugars. I know that using five onions is showing off, and although the dimension of different flavors from a single theme is intriguing, don't feel bound by it. Use one kind of onion if you prefer. The results are still great.

Ingredients

1 medium leek
½ white onion
2 shallots
1 small red onion
1 Vidalia or Walla Walla onion
¼ cup olive oil and 2 tablespoons
2 tablespoons balsamic vinegar
1 pound large white mushrooms
1 teaspoon garlic, minced
1 tablespoon dried thyme
¼ cup dry white wine
¼ cup vegetable stock

Yields: 2 to 4 servings

Rinse the leek, chop all the onions, and spread them on a roasting tray. Drizzle them with the ¼ cup olive oil and the balsamic vinegar. Put the tray, uncovered, in a 350° oven and roast the onions for about 20 to 30 minutes or until they are have caramelized and become a little crispy and sticky.

Meanwhile, slice the mushrooms. In a skillet, heat the 2 tablespoons of olive oil and then add the mushrooms, garlic, and thyme. The mushrooms will soak up the oil, but be careful not to add more because they will soak up additional oil as well that will be released later on, giving you an unpleasantly greasy dish.

Sauté the mushrooms for about 2 minutes to get a nice toasty flavor into them. Next, removing the pan from the heat, add the white wine and deglaze the mushrooms. Return the pan to the heat and let the alcohol cook out for about 1 to 2 minutes. Then, stir in the stock and cover the mushrooms. Reduce the heat, and simmer for 4 to 5 minutes, depending on the size of the mushrooms.

If you have good, fresh mushrooms, they will have dropped a lot of water and you now have a beautiful broth in the pan. If you bought dry, older mushrooms, shame on you! Just add a little water or broth and you should be okay.

Fold the onion confit into the simmered mushroom mixture, let the flavors meld for 1 minute, and then serve.

Roasted Root Vegetable Mash

Winter is a great time for root vegetables. They are always good, but I think that in the winter, they are something special. This recipe features celeriac or celery root. If you haven't tried it yet, you're missing out! It's a delicious vegetable with a complex taste and wonderfully smooth texture.

Ingredients

1 potato
1 large celeriac
3 carrots
3 parsnips
1 small beet
2 quarts of water
Olive oil (to drizzle over the vegetables)
Salt and pepper to taste
1 teaspoon fresh thyme, chopped
1 pat of soy margarine

Yields: 2 to 4 servings

See photo on page 130

Preheat your oven to 450°. Peel and chop the celeriac, potato, carrots, parsnips, and beet. Boil 2 quarts of salted water and blanch the vegetables for about 3 minutes (or until just after the water has returned to a boil.)

Drain the vegetables and lay them out on a roasting tray. Drizzle them with olive oil and sprinkle with salt and pepper. Cover the tray with foil and roast the vegetables at 450° for about 20 minutes. Check them periodically to make sure they are soft, but not mushy.

When finished, place the roasted vegetables in a bowl. Add the fresh thyme and soy margarine to the vegetables and mash them with the back of a large fork or potato masher until blended. How about these colors!

Butternut Squash Mashed Potatoes with Corn Gravy

I was inspired to create this dish by the beautiful month of November. Of course, Thanksgiving is an icon of tradition in America, but how about a funky, new concept that everyone can enjoy to liven up the table. I think you will like the corn gravy, and by using its natural starch, we have a whole new dimension on the palate, rather than a traditional, flour-thickened stock.

Ingredients for Potatoes

1 butternut squash, halved and cleaned
4 medium yukon gold potatoes, peeled and chunked
Salt and pepper to taste
2 tablespoons olive oil
2 ounces fresh herbs, chopped (parsley and thyme work well)
1 tablespoon fructose or brown sugar
Soy margarine (optional)

Ingredients for Corn Gravy

½ onion, chopped
3 garlic cloves, chopped
2 tablespoons olive or canola oil
24 ounces frozen cut corn
2 ounces white wine (chardonnay or chablis work well)
1½ cups vegetable stock
1 teaspoon dried sage
1 teaspoon dried thyme
1 teaspoon dried paprika

Yields: 4 servings

Rub oil, salt, and pepper on the butternut squash to coat and roast it in a 450° oven until tender. Meanwhile, boil the potatoes until tender.

At the same time, in another pan, prepare the corn gravy by sautéing the onion and garlic for 2 minutes in oil. Next, add the corn (frozen or thawed) and continue to brown. Add the white wine and reduce by half. Then, add the stock, sage, thyme, paprika, and simmer 3 minutes . Blend the corn mixture in a food processor for about 2 minutes and pour the mixture in a mesh strainer with a bowl underneath. Using a rubber spatula, push the mixture through until only the dry corn kernel skins are left. Discard the corn in the strainer. The gravy is in the bowl. Check for salt and pepper seasoning. Set aside or keep warm until ready to serve.

Drain the potatoes when they are finished. When the butternut squash is cool enough to handle, peel or cut off the skin. Then, with a masher or large fork, roughly mash the squash, potatoes, fresh herbs, oil, and fructose. For a smoother consistency, add a small amount of your favorite soy margarine.

Garlic & Sage Mashed Potatoes

Here are two great flavor compliments to potatoes. First, we'll pan roast the garlic to give it a sweet, nutty taste, which will meld with the sage flavor perfectly. I much prefer dried, ground sage in this application. I don't care much for fresh sage, but even if you do, I would still recommend using the dry variety because the fresh herb will be too pungent for this delicate flavor balance.

Ingredients

2 pounds potatoes (about 4 large potatoes)
2 tablespoons olive oil
2 tablespoons garlic, chopped
¼ cup white wine
1 tablespoon dried ground sage
1 tablespoon soy margarine
½ cup vegetable stock
1 teaspoon salt
1 teaspoon pepper

Yields: 4 to 6 servings

Peel and boil your favorite potatoes until tender. Don't use baking potatoes; they have too high a starch content.

Coat a small sauce pan with the olive oil. When it starts to get a little hot (don't let it smoke), add the chopped garlic. Just when the garlic starts to brown, remove the pan from the heat, and add the white wine. Return the pan to the heat and reduce by half for about 2 minutes. Add the sage.

When the potatoes are done, drain them and place them in a large bowl with the garlic mixture, soy margarine (CTF by not using margarine), stock, salt, and pepper. Mash the potatoes, adding a little more soy margarine or stock as needed, depending on the starch content of the potatoes.

Cajun Mashed Potatoes

Here's a great way to zing up potatoes. The flavor is robust, and the heat is mild.

Ingredients

2 pounds potatoes (about 4 large potatoes); peeled and chunked

2 teaspoons sherry wine

2 tablespoons quality Dijon mustard

2 tablespoons hot sauce

2 teaspoons fructose

1 teaspoon Cajun Spice blend (see the *Getting Started* section)

1 teaspoon seafood seasoning

2 tablespoons olive oil

1 cup vegetable stock

Salt to taste

Yields: 4 to 6 servings

Boil the potatoes until tender. Meanwhile, simmer the sherry wine so that the alcohol cooks out. Set aside.

Drain the potatoes when they are finished and place them in a large mixing bowl, combined with the reduced sherry mixture, Dijon mustard, hot sauce, fructose, Cajun Spice blend, seafood seasoning, oil, and vegetable stock. Add salt to your taste, but not pepper. There is already enough pepper in your spice blend.

With a masher or large fork, mash the potatoes to a smooth consistency. You may need to add more stock, depending on the starchiness of your potatoes.

New Mexican Rice

When I dine on Mexican food, I like a nice big bowl of rice, perfectly cooked, to carry the flavors of my meal. Cook your favorite rice and use this as the seasoning recipe.

Ingredients

¹/₃ cup red bell pepper, finely chopped

¹/₃ cup green bell pepper, finely chopped

¹/₃ cup yellow bell pepper, finely chopped

2 tablespoons powdered vegetable broth or
    2 small bouillon cubes

½ teaspoon cumin

1 teaspoon granulated garlic

1 teaspoon granulated onion

1 teaspoon salt

1 teaspoon paprika

2 cups uncooked rice of your choice

Yields: 4 to 6 servings

Add the chopped peppers and vegetable broth to your boiling rice water (before you add the rice). Then, add all the spices. Finally, add your rice and cook it as you normally would. The results are remarkable for such a simple and easy seasoning preparation.

Curry Coconut Rice

This recipe includes one of the most beautifully aromatic spice blends in the world—garam masala. Like curry, it is a spice blend from India, which is a little on the sweet side since it contains cinnamon, cloves and cardamom. Use it sparingly, but by all means use it.

Ingredients

2 teaspoons curry powder

1 teaspoon garam masala

2 tablespoons powdered vegetable broth or 2 small bouillon cubes

Salt to taste

2 cups uncooked rice (jasmine or basmati are superb in this recipe)

½ cup coconut milk

1 teaspoon sesame oil

1 teaspoon fructose

A few teaspoons fresh cilantro or mint, chopped

Yields: 4 to 6 servings

Add the curry powder, garam masala, and vegetable broth to your boiling rice water (before you add the rice). Then, add the salt. Finally, add your rice. About halfway through the cooking process, stir in the coconut milk, sesame oil, and fructose. Garnish with your chosen fresh herb.

Island Rice

Here is a simple, spiced rice that goes so well with tropical dishes or BBQ. The chopped mango with the Island spices is a perfect match.

Ingredients

2 tablespoons Island Spice blend (see the *Getting Started* section)

2 tablespoons powdered vegetable broth or 2 small bouillon cubes

2 cups uncooked rice

½ fresh mango, chopped

Yields: 4 to 6 servings

Add the Island Spice blend and vegetable broth to your boiling rice water. Then, add the rice. About halfway through the cooking process, stir in the mango.

Mediterranean Rice

I always think of Southern France, Spain, and Italy when I think of Mediterranean food and flavors. This rice is an herby, fresh interpretation of Spanish rice.

Ingredients

½ cups leeks, chopped
½ red bell pepper, minced
¼ cups of your favorite olives, minced
1 teaspoon garlic powder
1 teaspoon dried thyme
1 teaspoon dried marjoram or oregano
2 tablespoons powdered vegetable broth or
    2 small bouillon cubes
Salt and pepper to taste
2 cups uncooked rice of your choice
Extra virgin olive oil (to drizzle over rice)
½ lemon, juiced
A few tablespoons fresh parsley, chopped
¼ cups cheese of your choice, crumbled or
    shredded (optional)

Yields: 4 to 6 servings

Add the leeks, celery, red bell pepper, and olives to your boiling rice water (before you add the rice). Then, add the garlic powder, thyme, marjoram or oregano, vegetable broth, salt, and pepper. Finally, add the rice to the water and cook it as you normally would.

When the rice is done, garnish it with the drizzle of extra virgin olive oil, lemon juice, and parsley. If you'd like, make it a celebration by adding some organic Mediterranean cheese, such as shaved parmesan, feta, or chèvre, or some shredded soy cheese.

Sautéed Baby Bok Choy with Pine Nuts

Bok choy has always been one of my favorite vegetables. Watch the leaves when cooking. Cook them just until they wilt and turn a deep green. The base of the boy choy will still be crunchy at this point. Baby bok choy is great to work with since you can serve the whole vegetable, which makes a beautiful presentation.

Ingredients

2 tablespoons olive oil

1 teaspoon garlic, crushed

¼ cup pine nuts

¼ cup orange juice

¼ cup water

4 heads baby bok choy
   (allow 1 whole head per person)

2 teaspoons tamari soy sauce

1 teaspoon toasted sesame oil

Yields: 4 to 6 servings

Heat the olive oil in a skillet and add the garlic and pine nuts, stirring until they start to brown. Add the orange juice and water, and bring to a boil. Add the bok choy and cover to steam for about 2 minutes. Uncover and add the tamari and sesame oil. Continue cooking until bright green. Remove from heat and serve immediately.

Guacamole

At Horizons, we make a very simple guacamole since we use it in so many different dishes. I love guac!. It's so delectable and creamy. Hass avocados (from Mexico or California) are far superior. No matter the type, always use avocados that give to the touch when pressed with the fingers. If they are somewhat on the hard side (never use them fully hard with no give) add an extra lime—the lime juice will help "cook" the avocados and make them tender.

Ingredients

2 ripe avocados
¼ cup onion, minced
¼ cup tomato, minced
1 large lime or 2 small limes, juiced
Salt and pepper

Yields: 4 servings

With a fork, mash the avocados to the consistency you like. Stir in the rest of the ingredients.

Variation for Authentic Mexican Guacamole: To the previous recipe, add 2 teaspoons of the green sauce (from Yucatan Tofu recipe on page 119) and a fiery, minced jalapeño.

Pico de Gallo & Other Salsas

I like a raw vegetable salsa that has been "cooked" in lime juice. My favorite way to do this is to hand cut the vegetables into tiny dice. It's a lot of work but the result is well worth the effort. If you like a more cooked taste to your salsa, then add some quality canned tomatoes or better yet roast down some tomatoes on your own (see Bouillabaisse on page 110 for instructions).

Ingredients

4 red plum tomatoes, finely chopped
½ red onion, finely chopped
1 red bell pepper, finely chopped
1 green chile (jalapeño or Anaheim), finely chopped
1 celery stalk, finely chopped
1 teaspoon salt
1 teaspoon pepper
1 squeeze of a lime
1 drizzle olive oil
1 pinch of cumin
1 pinch paprika

Yields: 4 servings

Add the ingredients to a large bowl and stir. Let site in the refrigerator for at least an hour before serving.

Tropical Salsa Variation: Follow the recipe above and add a diced mango, papaya, and pineapple or any combination. Always use fresh fruit. If the fruit is under-ripe, the lime juice will soften it, but not make it particularly sweet, so add some fructose (about 1 teaspoon per whole fruit to compensate).

Roasted Corn Salsa Variation: We used to always have this on the menu—its so good you can eat a bowl of it as a salad. Lay out an 8- to 12-ounce frozen bag of frozen corn on a roasting tray. Drizzle with a little oil, sale & pepper. Roast at 550° for about 15 minutes until the top of the corn is just turning golden. Add to the salsa and chill. Alternative and better yet, roast corn on the cob or grill it with the husk on or off (if the husk is off, be careful the corn will cook and scorch fast. Then take a sharp knife and cut down the cob, taking off the kernels.

Black Bean & Corn Salsa Variation: Follow the Roasted Corn Salsa recipe and add some canned black beans (make sure to rinse them first).

Mango Avocado Relish

This is a great salsa-type topping for Cajun Grilled Tofu—a perfect summer dinner or light lunch. It also is a great topping for sandwiches and Mexican food, like burritos or tacos.

Ingredients

1 ripe mango, diced

1 ripe (but still firm) avocado, diced

¼ onion, minced

¼ green bell pepper, minced
     (or if you like heat, use a chile pepper)

Salt and pepper to taste

Juice of 1 lime

Yields: 2 to 4 servings

Place the mango, avocado, and onion in a mixing bowl. Add the bell or chile pepper. Sprinkle with salt and pepper. Drizzle the lime juice over the entire mixture and toss lightly with a spoon. Don't stir it too long or the mixture will lose its chunky consistency.

Vegan Chipotle Crema

This is a great dip or sauce to go with seitan wings or grilled portabella mushrooms. A chipotle is a smoked jalapeno pepper, so it provides a nice shot of heat and an incredible dimension of flavor. You can buy them dried and reconstitute them in warm water for 20 minutes, or buy them canned in adobo sauce.

Ingredients

2 chipotles

1 garlic clove

¼ cup onion, chopped

¼ cup tomato, chopped

1 tablespoon fructose

Salt and pepper to taste

1 tub soy cream cheese (or 12 ounces vegan
    mayo, which will give a thinner end result)

¼ cup olive or canola oil

Yields: 4 to 8 servings, depending on use

Rinse and remove the seeds from the chipotles and place them in the food processor or blender, along with the garlic, onion, tomato, fructose, salt, pepper, and soy cream cheese or vegan mayo. Blend the ingredients for 1 to 2 minutes until it reaches a smooth consistency. With the food processor or blender still running, drizzle in the olive or canola oil until thickened.

Cucumber Avocado Dip

Another fantastic seitan wing dip, this one is cool and refreshing, hinting Mexican. It's so simple to make. The only drawback is that the avocado will oxidize after a day in storage and turn the dip gray. It will still taste good, but if you plan to store it for a few days, leave the avocado out and substitute extra cucumber.

Ingredients

1 cucumber, peeled, seeded and chunked
1 avocado, peeled and seeded
1 cup vegan mayo
1 tablespoon Dijon mustard
1 teaspoon fructose
3 tablespoons olive oil
    (any variety, except extra virgin olive oil)
Salt and pepper to taste

Yields: 4 servings

In a food processor or blender, combine the cucumber and avocado. Add the vegan mayo, Dijon mustard, fructose, olive oil, salt, and pepper. Blend the ingredients for 1 to 2 minutes until it reaches a smooth consistency.

Top: Black Bean & Rice Griddle Cake (page 80)
Bottom: Stuffed Artichoke Bottoms New Orleans (page 69)

Left: Smoked Tofu Island Cocktail (page 70)

Top Right: Cuban Nachos (page 76)

Bottom Right: Seitan Skewers with Curry BBQ Sauce (page 67)

Top: Roasted Peppers with Caramelized Onions, Olives & Capers (page 78)

Bottom: Atlantic Tofu Gratin (page 73)

The Tropical Experience

....

*When I was young, my parents went on a weeklong cruise to
the Caribbean. My sisters and I were left with a house sitter, a map,
and an itinerary of where they were going.*

*As the days passed, using the map they left, I would follow their
route on the map as the ship went to mysterious and exotic-
sounding places, such as Trinidad, Martinique, and Barbados. I was
in love with how the names of these islands sounded as the visions
of blue waters and soft sands, wild tropical fruits, and exotic music
danced through my overactive imagination. This was my first
connection with the tropics.*

*When we were growing up, my mom was a travel agent, so our
house was always buzzing with travel talk. She would take us to
trade shows, where we would load up on every sticker, button, pin,
pen, and postcard that we could get our hands on.*

*For a few years, our entire breakfast room was covered in travel
posters for wallpaper, ceiling and all. We would eat our meals in a
room splashed with travel images from around the world.*

*My first island was Bermuda. About the same latitude as the
Carolinas, Bermuda is not as reliably tropical year round as some of
its southern neighbors, but it was spring, and the island was
immersed in an explosion of blooming flora. I will never forget the*

hotel gardens, grottoes, caves, views of the ocean from the restaurant and, of course, the pink-sand beaches.

When I was 15, we went to Mexico. Acapulco is made of a series of coves within mountains; the water is calm and bathtub warm. When the rest of my family went to the pool, I stayed in the ocean; when I wasn't in the ocean, I would gaze out at it from the beach. When the afternoon rains came, I would stay in the water and watch the giant clouds creep over the mountains on one side of the bay. Cold rain fell on me in the warm ocean, and I loved every second of it. The clouds would then drift up and over the other side of the bay mountains and disappear, leaving nothing but the hot sun shining on one young man in his new found paradise.

I will never forget the lively mariachi, the authentic Mexican food, and the beautiful sunsets.

I parasailed high over Acapulco bay, and as I peered out over the big, white high-rise hotel roofs, I caught glimpses of the real Mexico, the life beyond the tourism.

It wasn't until some 15 years later that I discovered the Mexico that I had really wanted to find. The village was known as Yelapa. It was about a half-hour powerboat ride from Puerto Vallarta, along the pacific coast. On the ride along the way, I passed palm jungles and little, thatch-roof communities and villages. The scenes are right out of a real-life Gilligan's Island. I arrived in a cove of impossibly blue water, and on the beach were huts and shacks, serving quesadillas, rice and beans, boiled chayote and carrots, and Mexican cerveza, but it was behind all this that I found my real Mexico.

I walked up the hillside paths among the palms. There on the small dirt trails were little stores and houses with smoke billowing from the kitchen windows; traditional Mexican music playing from porches; chickens, lizards, dogs, and donkeys wandering the streets; and a short distance away, a waterfall cascading down a towering rock face—a far cry from Acapulco. A tribute to my memory, the Yelapa Quesadilla was on the Horizons menu for two years.

I had done some tropical traveling on my own in the early days of Horizons Café. One year, I spent a Christmas in Key West. I drove the whole span of A1A from Miami to mile marker 0. It was just me in a convertible in late December, with the sun beating down on me. When I arrived in Key West, I was tired and sunburned, but as I walked around, I was re-energized by this wild and colorful tropical fantasy of a town. If a place must be touristy, it should be like Key West, with so much history to be celebrated. At night, the whole town gathers on Mallory Square dock to celebrate the sunset. It's a giant party as the sun sinks slowly into the sea. There are craft stands, music, and food, and sailboats cruise by in the background. I think there is something just so inspiring about a community that celebrates such a simple miracle, like the sunset, with a party each night.

Walking around that night, I read a menu at a restaurant by the docks that had a fish dish with sautéed bananas, peaches, pineapple, and mango in an amaretto butter sauce. Sound good? It became a Horizons tofu dish for many months as did lots of other tropical inspirations from that trip. I was incorporating more and more fruit and tropical spices into my dishes as well as exotic chilies, beans and rice, and citrus juices.

Later that year, I ventured to the US Virgin Islands. I stayed in St. Thomas; my hotel had a veranda with a breathtaking view of St. John in the background. You cannot fly to St. John; you must take a boat ride there as most of the island is a United States national *park. St. John is paradise if I have ever seen it. The beaches are unbelievable—Cinnamon Bay, Hawks Nest Bay, Trunk Bay— all picture perfect. I swam a lot, my mind in hyper-drive with inspirations for tropical dishes to serve at the restaurant. I rented a jeep and drove around the island, taking in the remarkable views. That night, back in St. Thomas, I sampled sauces at the hotel's restaurant like mango teriyaki and passion fruit hollandaise. I'll never forget how inspired I was trying these fruit-infused classics in a tropical setting. I took back many ideas that day; my menu was becoming more and more sun-splashed with these new ideas from my travels. The music was changing too; jazz and acoustic guitar music was giving way to steel drums and salsa.*

Since then I have been to over 30 tropical mainland and island destinations.

When it came time to expand the restaurant in 2001, I looked to the tropics to inspire a whole new dining experience for our guests. I didn't want a specific direction, like Mexican, Jamaican, or South American. I wanted the new restaurant to celebrate all the tropics—from the south pacific to coastal Spain, Africa, and Brazil.

So now, some nine years into the Horizons experience, the tropical rhythms flow strong. You will find many dishes with sunny inspirations on our menu, along with lots of classics. Our menu changes monthly so that our dishes have a freshly inspired feel to them. And when we come back from a trip, just look at the menu, and you'll know where we've been.

RSL
41º North Latitude (Home)
June 2003

Entrées

. . . .

Here is a selection of main dishes, spanning almost 10 years of Horizons. They have been adjusted and made "home friendly." Many contain their own sauce, side, vegetable, starch, or garnish, but feel free to explore outside the guidelines provided in this cookbook.

Match your own starches and vegetables, make an adjustment in a recipe that reflects your taste, giving it your own special touch. Let these be your dishes!

Kate and Rich toast the conclusion of the cookbook's last photo session as they are surrounded by the day's prepared entrées. The tropical inspiration surfacing in both the food and the atmosphere makes Horizons a true celebration for everyone.

Wild Mushroom Bouillabaisse

The mere mention of the word "bouillabaisse" conjures up romantic visions of the Provençal country and seaside, the aromas of saffron and fennel perfuming the table area, while fields of lavender float their soft scents by... Here is my tribute to this world-famous classic. Rouille, a red pepper spread, is the traditional garnish. For the best effect in this dish, I recommend pre-grilling some of your mushrooms. Slice portabella mushrooms into strips, cut large buttons in half, and leave smaller mushrooms whole—this is what will make the dish remarkable.

Ingredients

4 tomatoes (plum or slicing tomatoes)
1 medium onion
Salt and pepper
¼ teaspoon ground fennel seed (or 1 small bulb of fresh fennel, thinly sliced)
1 pinch saffron threads
½ cup white wine
2 tablespoons olive oil and more oil for sautéing the mushrooms
3 garlic cloves, crushed or sliced
2 pounds assorted mushrooms of your choice
2 cups stock (Don't use mushroom stock. It doesn't give contrast, and it doesn't let the mushrooms shine.)
1 tablespoon fresh thyme
2 roasted red peppers (jarred or canned is fine, or roast them yourself if you have the time)
¼ cup bread crumbs
Extra virgin olive oil (to make the rouille)
A few toasted baguette croutons

Yields: 4 servings

See photo on page 134

Cut the tomatoes into quarters and, cut the onion into julienne strips (think strips going against the ring lines). Spread these vegetables out on the a roasting tray, season with salt, pepper, fennel (or if you like fennel, use fresh, sliced very thin), and saffron threads. Pour the white wine into the bottom of the roasting tray, and then drizzle the olive oil over the top of the vegetables. Roast the dressed vegetables in a very hot oven (about 450° to 500°) for about 15 to 20 minutes or until the tops of the vegetables are slightly charred. Then, let them cool to the touch and peel the tomato skins, which should slip right off.

In a very large pan or casserole dish, sauté your mushrooms (fresh or pre-grilled) in oil with the garlic. When the garlic starts to brown, add the stock. Then, add the roasted tomato mixture, and simmer gently for 5 to 10 minutes, adding the thyme towards the end.

Meanwhile, in a food processor, combine the roasted red peppers with the bread crumbs, salt, pepper, and enough extra virgin olive oil to make a thick rouille. Spread the finished rouille on toasted baguette croutons as garnish to each bowl.

Roasted Portabella Mushrooms with Braised White Beans

This dish is a tribute to rustic French country cooking. It's a kind of cassoulet. In fact, you can add vegetarian sausage to the white beans for an extra meaty touch. The earthy mushrooms and creamy white beans in this arrangement are the setting for a nice autumn meal at home. Rake some leaves first or go for a walk in the October blaze of color. Then, come home and have this dish. That's the full effect.

Ingredients

4 large portabella mushroom caps
½ cup olive oil
1 teaspoon black pepper (preferably freshly ground)
3 tablespoons tamari soy sauce
1 tablespoon balsamic vinegar

Yields: 4 servings

Refer to page 81 for the ingredients and directions for *Braised White Beans*. To prepare the *Roast Portabella Mushrooms*, preheat your oven to 400°, and place the mushrooms on a roasting tray. Set aside.

In a small bowl, blend the olive oil, pepper, soy sauce, and balsamic vinegar. Thoroughly rub the mixture on the portabella mushrooms, and then bake them until they are soft to the touch. Be sure to check the mushrooms every 3 minutes. Depending on their thickness, the baking time could take anywhere from 6 to 12 minutes.

Serve the mushrooms over a serving of the white beans and with a nice green vegetable. Fresh spinach or salad greens also go well with this dish.

Tip: When roasting or grilling mushrooms, its important to take them off the heat just as they are starting to soften. They will keep cooking as they sit. Also, remember to save the mushroom juices for future stock bases.

Holiday Portabella

This is a recipe from the restaurant's late-Fall 2000 menu. The winter season is a festive time when we tolerate cold weather, large family gatherings, and holiday commercialism, and we make a celebration out of it all. Many vegetarians turn to seitan or mock chicken, which is great, but here's a recipe using meaty portabella mushrooms as the main course.

Ingredients

2 large portabella mushrooms
Olive oil for rubbing on the mushrooms and
    1 tablespoon to sauté the vegetables
Salt and pepper
½ small onion, chopped
1 tablespoon garlic, crushed
1 teaspoon ground dried sage
¼ cup dry white wine
1½ cups stock
1 tablespoon flour
1 teaspoon fresh rosemary, chopped
1 teaspoon fresh thyme, chopped
4 tablespoons toasted pumpkin seeds
4 tablespoons sun-dried cranberries

Yields: 2 Servings

See photo on page 132

Begin with cleaned portabellas. Brush them with olive oil, and sprinkle with salt and pepper. Use your fingers to rub the oil in. Roast in a 450° oven for about 10 minutes or until the mushrooms are tender. Remove the mushrooms from their roasting tray and set them aside in a bowl with any liquid that collected in the tray.

Next, in a sauté pan, heat 1 tablespoon of oil, and cook the onion and garlic with the sage and some salt and pepper to taste. Continue to sauté until the vegetables start to brown.

When the vegetables have browned, deglaze with the white wine and allow it to reduce by half before adding 1¼ cups of stock. Save the other ¼ cup of stock for the slurry.

Add the mushrooms and their juices that you reserved from the roasting tray to the stock mix in the sauté pan. Combine the flour with the remaining ¼ cup stock and stir thoroughly, making sure there are no lumps. Slowly drizzle the slurry into the pan while stirring constantly so that it creates a loose, buttery-type consistency. Bring to a bubble to cook the flour, then turn off the heat.

Stir in the rosemary and thyme at the last minute. Serve this dish with the toasted pumpkin seeds and sun-dried cranberries.

Tofu or Seitan & Wild Mushroom Pot Roast

This is a simple and satisfying dish that doesn't require a lot of "hands-on" preparation. The aromas of this roast will fill your house, and captivate anyone who is lucky enough to walk in while it's cooking. The glory of this production comes when you peel off the aluminum foil, and the beautiful dish of seitan or tofu with wild mushrooms shines before you, still simmering in its juices.

Ingredients

1 pound seitan or tofu chunks

½ pound of your favorite wild mushrooms, such as portabellas, chanterelles, and oysters

3 cups assorted vegetables, such as carrots, parsnips, zucchini, or cabbage

2 shallots or 1 onion, chopped

3 garlic cloves, chopped

2 sprigs fresh rosemary

2 sprigs fresh thyme

¼ cup olive oil (CTF by not adding any)

Salt and pepper to taste

½ cup stock

¼ cup Madeira or Marsala Wine

Yields: 2 to 4 servings

See photo on page 136

In a mixing bowl, toss the seitan or tofu, vegetables, herbs, and spices with the olive oil, salt and pepper.

Lay the ingredients in a baking dish. Pour the stock and the Madeira or Marsala wine around the bottom of the pan. Cover tightly with aluminum foil and bake it in a 450° oven for 45 minutes.

Peel back the foil carefully and taste the dish for salt, adding more if needed. Baste the seitan or tofu and vegetables with the liquid. Return the baking dish to the oven to cook, uncovered, for another 10 to 15 minutes.

Baked Tofu with Horseradish Crust & Roasted Red Pepper Sauce

Here's a simple-to-prepare dish with elegant results. Using baked or smoked tofu is a terrific shortcut to great flavor and texture. I think the flavor of horseradish and the texture of baked or smoked tofu pair beautifully in any preparation.

Ingredients

2 tablespoons prepared horseradish

½ cup bread crumbs (or croutons)

½ onion minced (¼ for the crust and ¼ for the sauce)

2 garlic cloves (1 clove for the crust and 1 clove for the sauce)

A few pinches of dried dill

A few pinches of fresh thyme

Salt and pepper to taste

1 teaspoon fructose

2 tablespoons extra virgin olive oil (1 tablespoon for the crust and 1 tablespoon for the sauce)

2 packs smoked or baked tofu fillets

4 roasted red bell peppers (recipe follows to make your own, or buy jarred or canned)

1 dash hot sauce

Yields: 2 Servings

The Crust

In a food processor or blender, place the prepared horseradish with the bread crumbs, ¼ cup onion, a garlic clove, and the first tablespoon of olive oil. Also add the dill, thyme, salt, pepper, fructose. Process until thoroughly combined. If your mixture is too thin, add some more bread crumbs. It should have a very thick consistency.

Spread the mixture on your tofu fillets and bake at 425° for about 15 to 20 minutes or until the crust solidifies and starts to brown.

The Sauce

Roast the red bell peppers with some olive oil in a 500° oven for 10 minutes or until they collapse. Remove from oven and set aside. When cool enough to handle, peel the skins and remove the seeds.

Next, in a food processor or blender, purée the roasted peppers with the second tablespoon of extra virgin olive oil, the second garlic clove, the hot sauce, the other ¼ cup onion, and a few more pinches of thyme. The sauce should have the consistency of salad dressing, thin enough to drizzle nicely.

For presentation, pour the sauce on the plate first, and then set the baked tofu fillets on top. Serve immediately.

Tofu Rancheros

So, who eats breakfast anymore these days? Or, should I ask, "Who makes breakfast anymore?" Well, here's a nice, tropical way to start the day with high-protein, scrambled tofu rancheros. Traditionally, rancheros are served on corn tortillas, but I like mine in a flour tortilla wrap. Guacamole and salsa work well as a garnish, but the authentic way to go is with the red sauce recipe included here.

Ingredients for Rancheros

1 (12- or 16-ounce) block of tofu

1½ tablespoons Cajun or Tropical Spice blend
(see the *Getting Started* section)

2 tablespoons olive oil

½ cup onion, chopped

½ cup bell pepper, chopped

2 vegetarian sausage links, chopped

½ cup vegetable broth

½ cup tomato, chopped

1 tablespoon soy margarine (optional)

¼ cup shredded cheese (optional)

Corn tostadas or flour tortillas

Various garnishes, such as green onion,
cilantro, lime, and avocado or guacamole
(optional)

Ingredients for Ranchero Sauce

½ cup red beans, rinsed and drained

1 cup roasted red peppers

1 garlic clove

2 teaspoons fructose

½ cup vegetable broth

2 tablespoons olive oil

Dash of cumin

½ teaspoon of paprika, salt, and pepper

Yields: 2 to 4 servings

See photo on page 133

About 30 minutes before cooking, crumble the tofu in a small bowl and mix with the Cajun or Tropical Spice blend.

Then, heat the olive oil in a skillet until it starts to ripple (almost smoking). Add the onion and bell pepper, and brown for about 3 minutes. Add the sausage and crumbled tofu and stir. Leave to brown for 1 minute, then stir again. Let the mixture sit on the heat for another minute.

Next, add the broth and tomatoes and stir. Let the broth fully absorb, and then stir in the soy margarine and cheese if you are using them. Turn down the heat to low.

For the red sauce, combine all the listed ingredients in a food processor or blender, and purée until smooth.

Finally, heat the sauce in a small saucepan, and warm the tostadas or tortillas in the oven for 3 minutes at 350°. Place the tofu mix over the tostadas or tortillas and top with the red sauce. Add your selected garnishes.

Grilled Tofu Salmon with Dill Sauce

I know many people who identify themselves as vegetarians and still eat fish every now and again. I still crave it myself every now and then, especially when at the Jersey or New England seaside or at Baltimore's Inner Harbor. This is a somewhat complicated dish, but the results are wonderful. Best of all, this dish is even better cold! Take it with you on a picnic or to the beach.

Ingredients for Tofu Salmon

1 garlic clove
½ shallot, peeled
1 tablespoon seafood seasoning
1 lemon, juiced
1 tablespoon fructose
¼ cup beet juice (fresh or use juice from a
    can or jar)
3 ounces quality Dijon mustard
2 ounces tamari soy sauce
½ cup olive oil
1 bay leaf
½ teaspoon dried thyme
1 (12- or 16-ounce) block of tofu, drained and
    cut into 3 slabs

Ingredients for the Dill Sauce

½ cup vegan mayo
1 shallot or ¼ cup onion, chopped
2 tablespoons quality Dijon mustard
1 teaspoon fructose
Salt and pepper to taste
½ cup cucumber, chopped (optional)
¼ cup cornichons or pickles, chopped
    (optional)
2 tablespoons fresh dill, chopped

Yields: 3 servings

See photo on page 135

The Tofu

In a blender, combine the garlic, shallot, seafood seasoning, lemon juice, fructose, beet juice, Dijon mustard, tamari, olive oil, bay leaf, and thyme. Blend until smooth. Marinade two of the three tofu slabs for at least two hours, or better yet, overnight. Store the third slab in water for later use in the sauce.

When the tofu has marinated long enough, grill it on an outdoor char grill. Turn the tofu once on each side to create crisscrossed lines. When you flip it, brush it with some more marinade so that it doesn't dry out. Let the grilled tofu rest a few minutes before serving with the dill sauce.

The Sauce

In a food processor or blender, combine all the items listed under *Ingredients for the Dill Sauce*, except the fresh dill. (Putting dill in a food processor or blender rips it up and makes it bitter.) Blend until smooth and then stir the chopped dill in by hand. Chill until ready to use.

Tofu Salmon with Vegan Wasabi Beurre Blanc

This recipe calls for the same grilled tofu salmon as prepared in the previous recipe, only this sauce is far more unique than the classic dill sauce. A true example of fusion, this dish pulls from rich and savory French decadent cuisine and shocks it with a fresh and spicy burst from the East. Use prepared wasabi from a tube or in the powder form, which you can reconstitute with water.

Ingredients

½ cup onion, chopped

2 tablespoons fresh ginger, chopped

2 tablespoons garlic, chopped

2 tablespoons canola or peanut oil

½ cup white wine

1 cup stock

2 tablespoons soy margarine (CTF by not using any)

2 tablespoons soy cream cheese

2 teaspoons tamari soy sauce

4 teaspoons fructose

3 tablespoons prepared wasabi

1 drizzle of toasted sesame oil

¼ teaspoon white pepper

2 tablespoons quality Dijon mustard

Yields: 3 servings

Sauté the onion, ginger, and garlic in the canola or peanut oil. When the onions are translucent, add the white wine and reduce to almost nothing. Add the stock and soy margarine. Simmer until the margarine melts.

In a blender, combine the above mixture with the soy cream cheese, tamari, fructose, wasabi, toasted sesame oil, white pepper, and Dijon mustard. Blend until smooth.

Grilled & Chilled Jamaican Jerk Tofu

One of my favorite things in the world is grilled and chilled tofu. It's texture is unbelievable! You'll love the spicy sweetness of the marinade too. Serve it as a sandwich or as an entrée with Hearts of Palm, Mango & Avocado Salad (recipe on page 52).

Ingredients

1 (12- to 16-ounce) block of tofu, drained
    and cut into 3 slabs
1/3 cup tamari soy sauce
2 tablespoons ketchup
1/3 cup canola or peanut oil
3 tablespoons Island Spice <u>OR</u> 2 tablespoons
    Cajun Spice (see the *Getting Started*
    section)

Yields: 3 to 4 servings

See photo on page 129

Place the three tofu slabs in shallow dish. Set aside.

In a small bowl, mix the tamari, ketchup, oil, and choice of spice blend. Pour the mixture over the tofu and marinate for at least one hour.

Have the grill very hot and ready for the tofu. Grill each side of tofu for about 2 to 3 minutes or until there are defined grill marks. While grilling, brush the tofu with the marinade, and be careful not to let it burn under a grill fire.

When the tofu is done, put it in the refrigerator to cool for at least 2 hours.

Yucatan Grilled Tofu with Green Sauce

The Yucatan Peninsula has entranced my imagination and spirit for years. Going there and experiencing the Mexican/Caribbean cuisine meld was one of my most cherished culinary adventures. Playa del Carmen and Isla Mujures are wonderful regions. You will almost always find a Yucatan-inspired dish on any Horizon menu. Here's one for you to try at home.

Ingredients for the Green Sauce

2 green bell peppers, chopped

4 tablespoons onion, chopped

2 garlic cloves, chopped

1 dash olive oil for roasting and 1 tablespoon for the sauce

1 bunch fresh cilantro

1 lime, juiced

Salt and pepper to taste

1 dash cumin

Ingredients for the Yucatan Tofu

1 (12- to 16-ounce) block of tofu, drained and cut into 3 slabs

½ cup oil

¼ cup tamari soy sauce

A generous amount of Mexican Spice or our Cajun Spice to marinate the Tofu slabs (see the *Getting Started* section)

A few lime wedges (for garnish)

Yields: 3 Servings

Green Sauce

Roast the green bell pepper, onion, and garlic with some olive oil in a 500° oven for 10 minutes. When cool, place roasted mixture in a food processor or blender, and purée it along with the cilantro and lime juice. Then, add the salt, pepper, and cumin. If your peppers are very bitter, compensate with a pinch or two of fructose or sugar.

The Tofu

Make the marinade by combining the oil, tamari and your choice of spice blends. Brush the three tofu slabs (about 5 ounces each) with the marinade. Grill each side of tofu for about 2 to 3 minutes or until there are defined grill marks.

When finished, set the grilled tofu over the green sauce, and perhaps over a small mound of basmati rice, which works excellently with this dish. Garnish with lime wedges.

Mediterranean Lemon Wine Sauce for Grilled Tofu

Wouldn't you just want to take two weeks on a small boat and cruise the Mediterranean, stopping at every island that you could find...and eating! Rhodes, Mallorca, Capri, Corsica, Sardinia—its' been a dream of mine for a long time. When I daydream down those waters, this dish comes to mind. A simple celebration of grilled tofu drenched in lemon, wine, and olive oil, and spiked with herbs.

Ingredients

1 (12- to 16-ounce) block of tofu; drained, cut into 3 slabs, and pre-grilled (see the *Getting Started* section)

2 tablespoons olive oil for sautéing

¼ cup leeks, chopped

2 garlic cloves, crushed or chopped

¼ cup dry white wine

1 lemon, cut into 3 wheels

¾ cup vegetable stock

Salt and pepper to taste

2 ounces your choice of fresh, chopped herbs, such as parsley, thyme, oregano or marjoram

1 tablespoon extra virgin olive oil

Yields: 3 servings

Heat the olive oil in a skillet until it starts to ripple (almost smoking). Add the leeks and garlic, and brown for about 3 minutes. Don't let the garlic scorch.

Add the white wine and let it reduce by half. Add the lemon wheels (no seeds) and the vegetable stock. Gently lay in the pre-grilled tofu fillets. Let the broth reduce by one-third. Then, add the salt, pepper, fresh herbs, and extra virgin olive oil. Simmer for 2 to 3 minutes.

Pan-Seared Tofu with Capers, Basil & Tomatoes

Here's another Mediterranean-inspired dish with more of a lean towards Italy. Pan-searing tofu gives it a golden outside layer, providing a much different effect than the grilled tofu. Capers are the pickled bud from a Mediterranean bush. To me, they have a snappy, almost mustardy taste. Just a few add so much dimension of flavor.

Ingredients

1 (12- to 16-ounce) block of tofu; drained, cut into 3 slabs, and pan seared (see the *Getting Started* section)

2 tablespoons olive oil for sautéing

1 red onion, slivered or finely chopped

2 tablespoons capers, drained

2 garlic cloves, crushed or chopped

¼ cup dry white wine

½ cup vegetable broth

Salt and pepper to taste

¼ cup fresh basil

1 cup plum tomatoes, diced

1 tablespoon extra virgin olive oil

Yields: 3 servings

See photo on page 136

Heat the olive oil in a skillet until it starts to ripple (almost smoking). Add the onion, capers, and garlic. Brown for about 3 minutes until the onions become translucent. Don't let the garlic scorch.

Add the white wine and let it reduce to almost nothing. Add the vegetable broth and let it reduce by one-third. Then, add the salt, pepper, basil, tomatoes, and extra virgin olive oil. Simmer for 1 to 2 minutes.

Prepare the pan-seared tofu. To serve, spoon the mixture over the tofu.

Variations: Add olives for another dimension of flavor. Or, add some chopped pine nuts to give the dish more of a pesto feel.

Pan-Seared Tofu with Peppers & Avocado Sauce

I made this dish for company one night. I bought an avocado for a garnish, but decided to cook it right in the sauce. I was amazed at how an avocado can add so much depth—all of the nutty, rich flavors came out and mingled with the sautéed peppers and the wine perfectly.

Ingredients

1 (12- to 16-ounce) block of tofu; drained, cut into 3 slabs, and pan seared (see the *Getting Started* section)

1 tablespoons canola or olive oil

½ red or yellow bell pepper, chopped

½ onion, chopped

3 garlic cloves, minced

A dash curry powder

1 relatively firm but ripe avocado, diced

¼ cup amber or dark rum or white wine

½ cup vegetable stock

½ cup scallions, chopped

1 tablespoon fructose

1 pinch salt

1 pinch pepper

Yields: 3 servings

Heat the olive oil in a skillet until it starts to ripple (almost smoking). Add the bell pepper, onions, and garlic, and sauté for about 2 minutes. Add the curry powder and avocado. Sauté for another 2 minutes. Remove from heat and add the rum or white wine. Return to the heat and reduce by half.

Still on high heat, add the stock, scallions, and fructose, and reduce by one-quarter or until slightly thickened. Add a pinch of salt and pepper. (Keep in mind that the tofu already has seasoning from the pan-searing).

Prepare the pan-seared tofu. Pour the sauce over the tofu. Serve with rice or rice and beans.

Blackened Tofu with Dirty Rice

Ah, New Orleans! French cuisine gone swamp crazy! You gotta love it when it's done right. I think a lot of people view this cuisine as spicy, sloppy, and unsophisticated, and in some cases, that may be true. But, true Creole cuisine is an art—a blend of French sophistication with Southern flavors and ingredients. Here I offer something a little more Cajun, which is the country cookin' of Louisiana, but with a Horizons cleanup.

Ingredients

1 (12- to 16-ounce) block of tofu, drained and cut into 3 slabs

Ample Cajun Spice blend to dust the tofu slabs (see the *Getting Started* section)

Canola or olive oil (enough to coat the bottom of the pan, and a little extra on hand in case the pan gets dry)

½ cup trinity, finely minced (equal parts of onion, green bell pepper, and celery)

2 cups precooked rice (white, brown, wild, or basmati—whichever you prefer)

½ cup stock

½ lemon, juiced (optional)

2 tablespoons fresh chive, chopped (optional)

Yields: 3 Servings

See photo on page 132

Coat the tofu generously (but not thickly) with the Cajun Spice blend. In a cast iron, aluminum, or stainless steel pan, bring the oil just to the smoking point. Use enough oil to rise one-quarter of the way up the side of the tofu slab once it would be placed in the pan. Don't worry: when working at a high enough temperature, the oil will simply cook the tofu. It will not be absorbed.

Slide the pan off the burner to avoid a grease fire, and very gently place the dusted tofu in the pan using tongs, a spatula, or a fork. Return the pan to the heat, and blacken the tofu, but don't burn it! This should take about 3 minutes. Remove the pan from the burner, gently flip the tofu, and blacken the other side. When blackened (not burnt), remove the tofu from the pan and set it aside in a warm oven. Pour out almost all the oil, leaving about 2 teaspoons in the pan (CTF by pouring out all the oil.) Add your minced trinity to the pan.

When the vegetables have begun to brown, add the precooked rice. Stir and sauté , adding about another 2 teaspoons of the Cajun Spice blend. After about 2 minutes, add the stock, and cook until the stock is absorbed.

Serve the tofu over the rice with lemon juice and fresh chives if you like.

Tofu Vera Cruz

When most Americans think of the Gulf, they think about the West Coast of Florida. On the other side of the water, on the East Coast of Mexico is a fascinating port city called Vera Cruz. It lies along the same latitude as Haiti and the Caymans. It's unique because it has more Spanish influence than most other Mexican cities, evidenced by the city's most famous dish, which is red snapper sautéed with tomatoes, peppers, capers, and olives. In our Horizons version, I add hearts of palm for color and texture. The hearts of palm lighten up the whole dish and makes a striking visual impression. This recipe provides the sauce for a pan-seared tofu.

Ingredients

1 (12- to 16-ounce) block of tofu; drained, cut into 3 slabs, and pan seared (see the *Getting Started* section)
1 tablespoon olive oil
¼ onion, chopped
¼ green bell pepper, chopped
2 ounces green olives, chopped
2 garlic cloves, chopped
1 teaspoon dried thyme
2 ounces white wine
1 ounce capers, drained
1 cup fresh tomatoes, diced
2 ounces hearts of palm, chopped
1 pinch saffron or 1 teaspoon paprika
6 ounces vegetable stock
1 lime, juiced
1 sprig fresh cilantro

Yields: 3 servings

See photo on page 131

Heat the olive oil in a skillet until it starts to ripple (almost smoking). Add the onion, pepper, olives, and garlic, and brown for about 2 minutes until the onions become translucent. Don't let the garlic scorch.

Add the thyme and then the white wine. Reduce to almost nothing. Add the capers, tomatoes, hearts of palm, saffron or paprika, stock, and lime juice. Simmer for about 5 minutes.

Prepare the pan-seared tofu. To serve, spoon the mixture atop the tofu and garnish with fresh cilantro leaves.

Grilled Seitan with Sage Mustard

In this dish, we will celebrate mustard. I absolutely love the stuff—all of it—even the yellow kind on my veggie dog! Here, we will blend mustard with what I feel are its two best herb compliments. Sage and rosemary were born for mustard. Try this dish, and I'm sure you'll agree as your taste buds carry your spirit down a cobblestone alley to a little, flower-adorned café in France in the spring. When grilling, beware of grill fires. They will burn your seitan and make it bitter. Simply move the seitan away from the fire or just squirt a little water on the fire.

Ingredients for Seitan

12 ounces of seitan (medallions, pieces, or preferably a steak); drained, rinsed, and patted dry
Olive oil for brushing the seitan
Salt and pepper to taste

Ingredients for Sauce

¼ cup quality Dijon mustard
⅓ cup olive oil
¼ cup water
1 tablespoon tamari soy sauce
1 teaspoon black pepper
1 teaspoon garlic, crushed
2 teaspoons dried sage
1 teaspoon fresh rosemary
1 splash white wine
¼ onion or 1 shallot, chopped
1 teaspoon fructose
1 pinch salt

Yields: 2 Servings, with ample marinade left-over to serve four using 24 ounces of seitan

Preheat your grill to medium. If you are using small pieces of seitan, you will have to skewer them. Be sure to soak the wooden skewers first for about 30 minutes.

Blend all the sauce ingredients in a blender until smooth. Brush the seitan with olive oil, sprinkle with salt and pepper, and lay it on the grill. Turn the seitan after about 3 to 4 minutes, depending on both the thickness of you seitan and the power of your grill.

Once you've turned the seitan, spoon the sauce over the topside of it, and let it "melt" onto the seitan. Grill another 3 to 4 minutes.

Seitan Steak Marsala

I love the idea of a Marsala dish. Marsala is a fortified wine from Italy that pairs so beautifully with mushrooms, garlic, and fresh herbs. This sauce is one of my favorites; it is deep, dark, and earthy—perfect for Autumn when you can use seasonal wild mushrooms to compliment the white mushrooms that I recommend here. This sauce also goes wonderfully with grilled tofu and vegetarian chicken products of all types.

Ingredients

16 ounces seitan (medallions, pieces, or preferably a steak); drained, rinsed and patted dry

3 tablespoons olive oil

1 tablespoon garlic, chopped

Salt and pepper to taste

8 ounces mushrooms, sliced (with some wild or exotic mushrooms as you please)

½ cup dry Marsala wine (Higher-grade Marsala comes in dry or sweet—use dry. Lower-grade Marsala, which is unlabeled in regard to dryness or sweetness, will work just fine here since we are reducing it.)

1 cup stock

1 teaspoon fresh thyme, chopped

½ teaspoon fresh rosemary, chopped

Slurry (1 tablespoon arrowroot powder or cornstarch mixed with 3 tablespoons broth or water)

Yields: 2 Servings

See photo on page 130

In a hot pan, sauté the seitan in hot olive oil. When brown (about 2 to 3 minutes), gently flip it over with tongs. Add the garlic to the side of the seitan and let it brown with the seitan in the oil. Add salt and pepper to taste.

When the garlic has started to brown, cover the whole pan with your sliced mushrooms. Remove from heat and pour in the Marsala. Return to heat and reduce the alcohol by half. Then, add the stock and fresh herbs. Bring to a boil.

When the mushrooms have cooked down, SLOWLY stir in the slurry. Boil for about 30 seconds—careful, any longer and the slurry will break.

Seitan French Dip

Growing up with 70's food, it's a wonder that we survived. My sisters would always order French dip when went out for lunch. I loved the concept. Here's another great way to use up your seitan bits and scraps. It's messy, but a real crowd pleaser. Try it!

Ingredients

1 quart dark mushroom or vegetarian beef
   stock
1 teaspoon garlic, crushed
1 teaspoon dried sage
1 teaspoon dried rosemary or 1 sprig of
   fresh rosemary
1 teaspoon dried thyme
2 cup seitan scraps, shredded
1 medium portabella mushroom, chopped
2 tablespoons oil
1 medium onion, julienned
½ cup sherry, Madeira or Marsala wine
3 to 4 French baguettes
Soy cheese, sliced or shredded

Yields: 3 to 4 servings

See photo on page 135

Bring the stock to a boil. Add the garlic, sage, rosemary, and thyme, shredded seitan scraps, and the portabella mushroom (buttons will also work, just substitute 1 cup).

Meanwhile, heat the olive oil in a sauté pan until it starts to ripple (almost smoking). Add the onion and brown until it is almost caramelized. Deglaze with sherry and continue cooking until it reduces slightly. Add the onions to the boiling broth and simmer for an additional 5 minutes.

To serve, slice open the baguettes and fill with your favorite cheese. Toast the bread to your desired doneness. Then, with tongs, lift the seitan out of the broth and place it in a roll. With a ladle, spoon some broth into a small soup cup and serve it on the side for dipping.

Grilled Seitan with Chimichurri

Chimichurri is a condiment hailing from Argentina. It's as popular there as ketchup is here. It's usually a combination of herbs, citrus, vinegar, and olive oil. This version, similar to the one that we serve at Horizons, is based around cilantro and mint, giving it an exotic, almost Indian touch.

Ingredients for Chimichurri

1 bunch cilantro (leaves only)
1 tablespoon fresh mint leaves
½ bunch fresh parsley (leaves only)
1 lime, juiced
¹/₃ cup olive oil
1 teaspoon salt
1 teaspoon pepper
¼ cup water
½ cup onion, chopped
2 to 3 garlic cloves

Ingredients for Seitan

12 to 16 ounces of seitan chunks, drained
   and rinsed
¹/₃ cup olive oil
1 tablespoon Tropical or Cajun Spice blend
   (see the *Getting Started* section)
2 tablespoons tamari soy sauce
1 teaspoon garlic, crushed

Yields: 2 servings

See photo on page 131

Place all the chimichurri ingredients in a food processor or blender and purée. Chill in the refrigerator for at least 20 minutes, preferably an hour.

Meanwhile, preheat your grill to medium. Place the seitan in a shallow dish and set aside. If you are using small pieces of seitan, you will have to skewer them. Be sure to soak the wooden skewers first for about 30 minutes. Marinade the seitan in the oil, spice blend, tamari, and garlic for 10 to 15 minutes before skewering.

When ready, grill the seitan for 7 to 8 minutes, turning at least once. Serve the seitan with the chilled chimichurri.

Grilled & Chilled Jamacian Jerk Tofu (page 118) shown with Curried Cucumber Rice Salad (page 56)
& Hearts of Palm, Mango & Avocado Salad (page 52)

Seitain Steak Marsala (page 126) shown with Roasted Root Vegetable Mash (page 87)

Top: Grilled Seitan with Chimichurri (page 128); bottom: Tofu Vera Cruz (page 124)

Top Left:
Holiday Portabella
(Page 112)

Bottom Left:
Blackened Tofu
with Dirty Rice
(page 123)

Right:
Tofu Rancheros
(page 115)

Wild Mushroom Bouillabaisse (page 110)

Top:
Seitan
French Dip
(page 127)

Bottom:
Grilled Tofu
Salmon with
Dill Sauce
(page 116)

Top: Pan-Seared Tofu with Capers, Basil & Tomatoes (page 121)
Bottom: Seitan & Wild Mushroom Pot Roast (page 113)

Reasons & Revolving Seasons

. . . .

The boat has cleared the docks. I push the throttle forward, and we are on our way. It's my birthday, and rather than do the "been-done" routine of going out to a restaurant, my family and I are taking a boat out onto Lake Nockamixon. Kate and I discovered the lake shortly after moving to Bucks County in the summer of 2002. It's just a little over 10 minutes from our house, and it's one of the most beautiful places I know. Having such great beauty so close to home is a very inspiring thing, especially when you love the seasons as much as I do. Nowhere are seasons more recognized than on a lake. We have been there in all seasons to celebrate with the lake.

To be in love with the changing seasons and in love with food is quite a wonderful dynamic. It goes far beyond living with the harvest. It is about what you need and love to eat through all the different moods, pastimes, and fashions that affect our lifestyle with the seasons.

‽

In the winter, I love stews or maybe a pot roast, where your main protein cooks closely with your vegetables and starch, and the flavors of all your ingredients mingle, bringing closeness, comfort, and warmth. The fire burns warmly, the snowflakes dance outside the window, and candles cast soft, shadowed lights on the walls of your home, your sanctuary. Top it off with red wine or hot chocolate and a long movie with a big blanket. These stews and roasted foods fill me in the winter. Long after the holidays have passed, I turn to my potatoes, carrots, seitan, rosemary, onions, and mushrooms to flavor my spirit on the long inner journey to spring.

CB

In spring, I am out in the garden. The windows are open during the day to let the life air into the house. I brush dirt away, looking for those first budding signs of my tiger lilies, sedum, coreopsis, and wild grass. The music changes; new age dreamscapes have given way to my high-school first loves of The Who, CSN, and the Dead. The sky is bluer, and the world is magically becoming greener. The spring vegetables will soon be in the farmers' markets: arugula, baby spinach, asparagus, and fennel. It's perfect weather for a hot-and-cold salad—a huge plate with a hundred vegetables and a slab of pan-seared tofu atop. How about a nice light pasta dish, simmered in vegetable broth with garlic and green onions, with all of those wonderful spring green vegetables cooked just perfectly. If we are lucky, spring lingers, it dances, it paces itself so wonderfully well that each day is not rushed, but savored with the life show that is exploding around us.

SO

Then summer hits, and like winter in the Northeast part of the USA, it hits hard. The trees have created a canopy of lush greens. There are more shades of green than you ever remembered or ever imagined possible. The shadows and secret paths in the woods take on a magical life, the birds swoop in and out of the tree tops, the crickets chirp at night, and the fireflies bring the stars to earth.

Quick, in a three-month period, you must get to the amusement parks, the shore, the mountains, on the road, find somewhere to swim, and get into shape. There are countless pressures in summer. Me, I just like to sit back and enjoy Mother Nature's show. I try to appreciate each day, to take a deep breath and a long look at the simple beauty of it all, because it is gone all too soon.

In the summer, there are two words that dominate my food life: Mexican food and grilling. Mexican food has always been my favorite, ever since I was very young. When Kate and I have company, we often just grill up vegetables like onions, peppers, zucchini, mushrooms, and asparagus, and set them on a huge platter. On another platter, we place avocado, marinated tomatoes, salsa, jalapenos, beans, cheese, and fresh cilantro. This my friends—sitting outside with a huge tortilla wrap stuffed with grilled vegetables and Mexican condiments with a side of rice and beans—is what it is all about. Combine it with a margarita and a sunset, and you have poetry.

❧

Then, sometime in late-August, you will feel it. You will be sitting on your porch or deck and it will come—the first breeze of autumn. You will know it right away. It does not touch and caress your skin; it blows into you and sometimes right through you. It is time. We still have a month and a half of green, but the weather will be much different. The rains come and the nighttime temperatures bring us inside. Then in mid-October, the miracle happens. The leaves turn color and the magic show begins.

In autumn, my palate becomes alive like never before. I go for deep flavor layers and intricate sauces with separate preparations and attentions to each vegetable, starch and main protein, all perfectly cooked and separately seasoned to compliment each other on a single plate. Basil gives way to rosemary and thyme, gazpacho gives way to *chowder, rum to wine, and tortillas to crusty rustic breads. Mushrooms are on my mind, stewed with Marsala wine and thyme and draped over roasted seitan or pan-seared tofu. Capers, olives, and mustard sauces as well as roasted pecans, hazelnuts, and walnuts garnish the dishes. Our minds wake up, just like when we went to school. It's time to think more, ponder, write and reflect. To sit by a window on a rainy October afternoon and listen to some soft piano music, coffee cup in hand. This is autumn. Before the holidays hit, I want a little time for me.*

Then they come. . . the holidays. Now it's really time to eat. Out-of-town family arrives; college kids are home; and reruns of Charlie Brown, Rudolph, and Frosty appear. It's a feast of clichés: soy turkey & gravy, stuffing, cranberry sauce, mashed potatoes, string bean casserole, and pumpkin pie. Familiarity breeds content. Outside, it's colder than you remember. The skies take on a fantastic, orange hue around 4:30 PM; you can almost smell snow in the air. The stars seemingly shine so much brighter at night, and we worship those evergreen conifers outside that provide us with green all season long. For me, it's the solstice, the real reason that I celebrate the holidays. The sun and earth have been doing this holiday ritual much longer than we have. The solstice is universal among us. There is no conflict of belief or myth. Our ethnic or geographic origin cannot separate us from earth's life cycles and seasons. We are in this together.

&⁊

We turn the boat around at the far end of the lake. It's June and the greens will be around for a while. I spot little inlets and trails along the shore that I want to explore next time. The mist from the water is so refreshing. The sunshine warms me from the inside out. My hands loosely on the steering wheel, I look at the beautiful scenery surrounding us. I look at my family surrounding me, and I smile as the docks come into sight. I slow the throttle. It's time to go home. . . for dinner.

Desserts

. . . .

Food has always been a source of excitement in my life. It is at once creative, thoughtful, nourishing, and symbolic. The actual preparing of food and sharing it with others is so much more than a simple means of refueling our bodies. It becomes a way that we interact socially and learn from one another. Most of our warmest memories are based around meals of some kind: baking cookies as kids, breakfasts in bed, romantic dinners, and holiday parties. What a wonderful way for people to connect!

These recipes provide a means for people to keep connecting without using animal products. Vegetarians are having an increasingly manageable time finding food to eat at just about any restaurant as society becomes more considerate of veggie lifestyles. Vegans, however, often remain socially isolated when it comes to sharing meals with many others.

Whether you're vegan or ovo-lacto vegetarian, keeping kosher, or watching your cholesterol, Horizons is able to accommodate everyone at once. At the restaurant, we serve food on a least common denominator: great taste. The social atmosphere of enjoying delicious food with the ones you love goes uninterrupted regardless of dietary commitments, preferences, or restrictions.

On the baking side of things, making desserts with no animal products continues to be both challenging and enlightening. It compels me to reinvent classic recipes, capturing traditional tastes and textures. At the same time, I am able to explore less familiar ingredients and techniques to create some new favorites.

Working alongside Rich in the kitchen has made all the difference in my experience as pastry chef at Horizons. His knowledge and skills are only surpassed by his keen culinary intuition. He begins with flavor combinations and works his way through regional influences and different techniques until he assembles a dish that is simply perfect from every angle. Working with him has inspired me to take that approach with my desserts.

What follows is a collection of recipes designed to do all the things that good desserts and baked goods should do: bring people closer together. . . to themselves, friends, family, and loved ones. These recipes accomplish this without any animal products, but with all the great taste. You will have to be more precise with measuring in dessert recipes than the cookbook's savory recipes to achieve certain results in baking. But once you understand the techniques, let your culinary imagination get the best of you, and springboard off these recipes to really make them your own.

Common Ingredients for Pastries

Agar (or Agar-Agar)
A thickening agent made from seaweed with very strong setting power. Like many other seaweed products, it is used more frequently in Asian cuisine than in Western cuisine, but it provides vegetarians with an excellent replacement for gelatin in mousses and other recipes. Available at most natural food stores, agar comes in the form of sheets, flakes, or powder.

Agave Syrup
A thick, sweet liquid sweetener. Agave syrup is obtained from the agave cactus and can be used as a one-to-one replacement for honey.

Arrowroot Powder
A thickening agent available at many natural food stores, this powder is obtained from the arrowroot plant and is believed to be more easily digested than other thickening starches, such as wheat flour or cornstarch. Arrowroot powder can be used as a one-to-one replacement for cornstarch.

Balsamic Vinegar
In vegan baking, acids are necessary to react with leavening agents in order to make cakes and others desserts rise. Balsamic vinegar is a potent vinegar with a 6% acidity. When used correctly, the taste is not detectable in the final product.

Baking Powder
Baking powder is a combination of baking soda and cream of tartar, which is used to bind and leaven baked goods. This is one ingredient that requires very careful measuring. Too much of it can result in dry, hard cakes or crusts.

Baking Soda
Sodium bicarbonate (baking soda) can be found in any supermarket or convenience store. Used in proper combination with other ingredients, baking soda will help dough and batter rise. Only use the amount listed in the recipe; otherwise, the final result may taste salty. Timing is also crucial when mixing baking soda with wet or liquid ingredients in order to get the most power from the amount of baking soda being used.

Egg Replacer

Found in most natural food stores, egg replacer is a powder made of different starches that, when combined with liquid, replaces eggs in many baking recipes. Whipped in a blender, it provides some of the volume attained by whipping egg whites. Mixed into a batter, egg replacer provides the setting and binding qualities needed to hold a cake together and make it rise.

Flour

We use all-purpose, unbleached, white-wheat flour at the restaurant. For making pastries, white-wheat flour far outshines whole-wheat flour because it's light and airy. Replacing one tablespoon of one cup of flour with one tablespoon of arrowroot powder or cornstarch yields the same result as using pastry flour, which has an even lighter finish. If you prefer whole wheat flour, by all means, use that instead of the white, or try combining whole wheat and white flour to cut down the grittiness of the whole wheat. On occasion, our customers request gluten-free cakes, which involves replacing wheat flour with combinations of other flours, such as potato, tapioca, or rice flour, and large amounts of cornstarch.

Fructose

Found at many natural foods stores, fructose is a granular sweetener derived from corn that looks, tastes, and works just like white sugar. It can be used as a one-to-one replacement for sugar in any dessert. It makes a wonderful caramel sauce, and it also works very well when ground in a coffee mill to make a "powdered sugar" garnish.

Margarine

Many people are uneasy with using margarine in their cooking. Some supermarket brands list whey among the ingredients, making them unusable for vegans. In addition, health-conscious people are wary of the many brands' hydrogenated oils, a process that alters the molecular structure of the oil, allowing it to remain solid at higher temperatures. The great news is that there are now both vegan and non-hydrogenated brands easily available. Be careful when selecting a brand; you will find that some work better for certain purposes than for others.

Oil, Canola

Canola oil carries very little flavor into a recipe. It is, therefore, an excellent way to add fat to your recipe without bringing additional flavors. There may be times when you might prefer to taste olive oil or sesame oil such as in a cake or crust; however, canola serves well as a neutral baking oil.

Salt

Just like sweetener is used in savory food, salt is used in pastries to enhance existing flavors. Salt brings out the buttery flavor of margarine in crusts. It also enhances the creaminess of whipped or chantilly cream and the natural flavors of any nuts.

Shortening

Vegan shortenings are available in most supermarkets, but you probably have to head to a natural foods store if you want to use a non-hydrogenated brand. Shortening works very well in combination with margarine and/or oil for crusts, and it is ideal for icing because of its durability and high-melting point.

Silken Tofu

Many types of tofu are available in supermarkets and natural foods stores: extra firm, firm, and soft. Chances are, these come packaged in water with a nearby expiration date. Silken is a special type of tofu made by an entirely different process where the soy milk actual forms into bean curd in the package in which it is shipped, sold, and eventually bought by you. The formed tofu is not pressed as much as other tofu, and it retains a larger percentage of soy whey, leaving it much moister. It comes in sealed, lined boxes, and it can sit on your shelf for months before you use it. I believe that silken tofu is not suitable as a base for mousse, icing, pudding, or anything of that nature, but I highly recommend using it to replace the creaminess and volume that eggs bring to traditional batter and dough recipes. When used correctly, the soy flavor is lost in the recipe, and all that is left is the texture.

Soy Milk

Having been a soy-milk drinker for a long time, I have grown to like the stuff. However, it was definitely a growing process, and I didn't just start liking it overnight. It took a great deal of me getting used to it in cereal and flavored coffee before I could ever think of drinking it straight. I can, therefore, certainly understand that someone accustomed to dairy milk may find the flavor offensive. For this reason, I am very selective in the soy milk I use, which is generally neutral in flavor and white in color. When you decide on a brand you like, it can be used as a one-to-one replacement for dairy milk.

Xanthan Gum

Xanthan gum is the key to making good sorbet. It is commonly used in salad dressings and many processed foods to suspend particles evenly throughout the final product. Along the same lines, when used correctly, it blends all the ingredients in sorbet evenly, leaving a perfectly creamy sorbet. Sorbet without xanthan gum is like crystallized ice; it melts into flavored water. Sorbet made with xanthan gum melts into a pool of rich juice—that is, if you don't finish it before it melts.

Yeast

Yeast is a wonderfully mysterious ingredient used in baking. Intimidating to many, it comes in so many forms, such as cakes or dry powders, and in different grades of power, such as quick-acting and double-acting. Working with it depends greatly on the heat and humidity in the kitchen. The higher the heat or humidity, the more powerful a reaction the yeast will give. I prefer working with the dry powders found at any supermarket.

Banana Macadamia Nut Cinnamon Buns

Rich and I went to brunch at a nearby restaurant/inn when we first moved to Bucks County, and I found myself bending the vegan rules, so to speak, to sample some cinnamon buns. I just had to make them for the restaurant. Here they are, sure to please and guaranteed to leave you feeling great to start the rest of your day.

Ingredients for Dough

4 cups flour
¾ cup fructose
1 teaspoon cinnamon
½ teaspoon salt
1 teaspoon baking powder
¾ teaspoon baking soda
1 teaspoon powdered yeast (about one package)
½ cup soy milk
4 tablespoons soy margarine, melted
½ cup water

Ingredients for Filling

½ cup fructose
2 teaspoons cinnamon
4 tablespoons soy margarine, melted
2 ripe bananas, sliced ¼-inch thick
¾ cup toasted macadamia nuts, crushed

Ingredients for Icing

4 tablespoons soy margarine
¼ cup fructose
1 very ripe banana
⅓ cup soy milk

Yields: 6 to 8 servings

See photo on page 160

Tip: If you don't serve the buns immediately, allow them to cool at room temperature and store in an airtight container in the refrigerator. When ready, heat them in the microwave (1 minute per bun) or a 350° oven for 10 minutes. Then, garnish with icing and toasted macadamia nuts.

In a large mixing bowl, sift together 1 cup of flour with fructose, cinnamon, salt, baking powder, baking soda, and yeast. Set aside.

In a small saucepan or in a microwave-safe dish, heat the soy milk, soy margarine, and water until the margarine is completely melted. Add the heated liquid to the dry ingredients and stir with a whisk or large spoon.

Add the rest of the flour, a little at a time, kneading as the batter turns to dough. When the dough is no longer sticky to touch, cover it with a kitchen towel and place it is a warm place for about 30 minutes to rise. It should double in size. After the dough has risen, preheat your oven to 350°. Then, roll out the dough on a floured surface to about ¼- or ½-inch thick.

To make the filling, combine the fructose, cinnamon, and melted soy margarine in a small mixing bowl. Spread the filling on top of the rolled dough. Then, cover the dough with the banana slices and the toasted macadamia nuts. Roll the dough up like a carpet, and slice it into about 6 to 8 buns, or smaller if you prefer to have more miniature cinnamon buns.

Bake the buns on a nonstick baking sheet for about 20 to 25 minutes, rotating tray once halfway through baking to ensure evenness. In the meantime, make the icing by combining the soy margarine, fructose, banana, and soy milk in a food processor and blend until smooth. Chill the icing in the refrigerator.

Remove the buns from the oven, smear with icing, and sprinkle with remaining macadamia nuts. Serve immediately.

U T Cornbread

My first introduction to Texas came in the form of a stop on a college tour when my brother first thought of attending the University of Texas in Austin. While most of our time was spent touring lots of Texas-sized campus buildings, I do have one outstanding food memory—cornbread with peach butter. I loved the extra touch of whole corn kernels in the bread. I've been a Texas-sized cornbread fan ever since. This is an excellent recipe for summer!

Dry Ingredients

1¾ cup cornmeal
1½ cup all-purpose flour
2 teaspoons baking powder
1 teaspoon baking soda
½ cup fructose

Wet Ingredients

½ cup canola oil
6 ounces silken tofu
4 tablespoons margarine
¼ cup agave syrup
1 cup soy milk
2 tablespoons BBQ sauce (optional)
¼ cup lemonade
1 cup fresh or frozen corn kernels

Yields: 6 to 8 servings

See photo on page 58

Preheat oven to 350. Grease a 9x11-inch baking pan with canola oil. Set aside.

In a medium-sized mixing bowl, sift together all dry ingredients. Then, blend together all wet ingredients in a blender. Pour the blended wet ingredients into the dry ingredients and mix with a spoon or whisk just until all ingredients are combined. Be careful not to overmix. The batter will be very thick. Stir in the corn kernels.

Pour the batter into the pregreased baking pan and put in the oven immediately. Bake for 35 minutes, turning halfway through baking to ensure evenness.

Remove from the oven. Cornbread can be served warm or at room temperature with salads, soups, and entrees, etc., or incorporated into a dessert.

Tart Tatin à l'Américain

I first made a tart tatin when I was about 14. Having two years of French under my belt, my parents picked up a pocket-sized cookbook of national French dishes for me. The recipe for traditional apple tart tatin included a little story about the two Tatin sisters who earned their living making this dessert in France centuries ago. In more recent years, I have sampled the tart tatin in cafés and brasseries throughout France, only to find it to be much more amber from caramelization than mine. The apples are sliced thinner and seem much less juicy. Maybe it is just my background of making American apple pies, but I greatly prefer my version. So for what it's worth, the following is my version: apples and pears baked in an oven-safe dish—not in an iron skillet—still flipped upside down in the end—but full of juicy apples.

Ingredients for Fruit

2 tablespoons soy margarine

1 tablespoon canola oil

4 tablespoons fructose

4 large apples; peeled, cored and sliced about ¼-inch thick

3 large pears; peeled, cored and sliced about ¼-inch thick

¼ cup cognac (optional)

Ingredients for Crust

2 tablespoon soy margarine

2 tablespoon shortening

1 cup flour

1 teaspoon arrowroot powder or cornstarch

2 tablespoons fructose

½ teaspoon salt

1 tablespoon canola oil

2 tablespoon cold water

Yields: 6 servings

See photo on page 163

Heat a large skillet on high heat. Add the soy margarine and canola oil. When the fats are melted and hot, add the fructose. Then, add the apple and pear slices, a few at a time so as not to drop the temperature of the pan.

Brown the slices on each side for about 1 to 2 minutes. Deglaze the pan with cognac and cook for another minute. Then, remove the pan from the heat and allow the apples to cool to the touch.

To make the crust, combine the margarine, shortening, flour, arrowroot powder or cornstarch, fructose, salt, and canola oil in a food processor and mix until crumbly. Then, add the cold water, a little at a time as you mix, until it starts to form a soft ball that is not sticky to the touch. Allow the dough to rest, covered in the refrigerator, for about 10 minutes. The trick to good workable dough is temperature. The fats have to cold in order to bond with the flour so the dough will roll out evenly without sticking.

As the dough rests, grease a 9-inch oven-safe pie pan with canola oil, and dust it with 1 tablespoon fructose. Then, arrange all the apple and pear slices in a tight circular pattern within the pie pan.

Next, roll the dough out on a floured cutting board to about ¼-inch thick. Using a large spatula or knife, transfer the dough onto the oven-safe dish. Cut the excess crust from the edges of the dish, and pinch the ends of the crust

(continued next page)

tightly to the edge of the pan. Pierce a few tiny holes in the top center of the crust to allow the heat to escape while baking.

Bake the tart for about 30 to 35 minutes or until the crust in crisp and golden brown. After the first 15 minutes, rotate the pan 180° to ensure even baking.

Remove the pan from the oven and allow the tart to cool for about 20 minutes. Then, invert it onto a plate. If any of the slices stick to the oven-safe dish, just pick them off and rearrange them onto the top of the tart.

Allow the tart to cool completely in the refrigerator for 1 to 2 hours. Serve the tart cold and garnish with powdered fructose, or finish it "American style" (heated in the oven for 5 minutes then topped with vanilla soy ice cream).

Mango Variation: Use 6 to 8 ripe mangoes and tequila instead of the apples, pears and cognac.

Plantain Variation: Use 6 large ripe plantains and rum instead of the applies, pears and cognac.

Winter Spiced Pear

When traveling through Poland during Christmas 2001, I was overwhelmed by the holiday sights and smells of dried citrus and clove. This recipe combines these flavors with an elegant presentation for a light and sophisticated dessert.

Ingredients

4 ripe pears, clean skinned
2 cups water
4 whole cloves
¼ teaspoon cinnamon
¼ teaspoon nutmeg
¼ teaspoon allspice
¼ cup fructose
2 blood oranges, cut in wheels

Yields: 4 servings

See photo on page 161

In a large saucepan, heat the water, cloves, cinnamon, nutmeg, allspice, and fructose on medium heat for 5 minutes. In the meantime, peel and core all 4 pears.

Place the pears in the simmering water, standing upright. Cover with a lid, and increase the heat to medium-high for about 10 minutes. Halfway through cooking, place half of the blood orange wheels in the simmering water. Remove the pears from the saucepan. Continue to reduce the liquid until it becomes thick and syrupy.

Place the pears on a dish and baste them in the blood orange, spice syrup. Garnish with the remaining blood orange wheels.

Unfried Ice Cream with Cruzan Bananas

Fried ice cream is a traditional Mexican dessert. While I remember indulging in it as a kid, the idea of it seems almost too rich now. Dairy ice cream, deep-frozen, rolled in corn-flake crumbs, flash-fried, and topped with whipped cream and honey! At Horizons, we've lightened up this classic favorite. Soy ice cream, rolled in crisp tortilla crumbs—so that you don't even need to fry it in order to get that crunchy crust—then topped with caramelized banana slices. It's still decadent and rich with the Cruzan sauce, Brazil nuts, and agave syrup, but you actually feel good after eating it! This dessert is quick and easy to make, and it's sure to impress any dinner guest.

Ingredients for Unfried Ice Cream

1 quart vanilla soy ice cream

2 tablespoons canola oil

4 ripe bananas, peeled and sliced on the bias
  into ½-inch chunks

¼ cup toasted Brazil nuts, crushed

4 tablespoons agave syrup

Ingredients for Tortilla Crush

4 cups whole tortilla chips, salted or unsalted

1 teaspoon cinnamon

2 tablespoons fructose

Ingredients for Cruzan Sauce

½ cup dark rum

¼ cup water

1 tablespoon fructose

1 tablespoon fresh lime juice

Yields: 4 servings

See photo on page 161

Remove the ice cream from the freezer, and allow it to soften for about 10 minutes. Meanwhile, in a food processor, combine all the *Tortilla Crush* ingredients and process until all chips are completely ground. Set aside. Next, in a small mixing bowl, combine all *Cruzan Sauce* ingredients and stir until the fructose is dissolved. Set aside.

Scoop 8 ice cream balls and roll them in the tortilla crush. Arrange the ice cream balls, two on each plate, and put them in the freezer while you make the bananas.

Heat a large saucepan on high heat with 3 tablespoons canola oil. When the oil starts to ripple, add the bananas, a few slices at a time so as not to drop the temperature.

Allow the bananas to brown on one side for about 1 to 2 minutes. Then, flip them and brown the other side for another 30 seconds. Deglaze the pan with the cruzan sauce, and cook for an additional minute until the sauce boils, the alcohol cooks off, and the rum and sugars caramelize on the bananas. Do not overcook the bananas or they will become mushy.

Lastly, divide the caramelized bananas evenly on top of each set of ice cream balls. Garnish each with toasted Brazil nuts and about 1 tablespoon agave syrup. Serve immediately.

Tropical Sorbets

Knowing how to make good sorbet is a very important skill to have in the kitchen. Not only is it much more rewarding to keep a quart of homemade, fresh sorbet around during the summer, but getting adventurous and coming up with fun flavors can be an excellent way to garnish desserts or offer more calorie-friendly dessert options to dinner guests. Once you know how to get the right texture, the possibilities are endless. It will be well worth the investment in an ice cream/sorbet maker if you do not already have one. Here are a couple tropical flavors to get you started. For mango, you'll be using the actual pulp of the fruit; for coconut, you'll use the milk; and for lime, you'll use the juice.

Ingredients for Mango Sorbet

1 tablespoon xantham gum

1 cup water

5 cups mango purée (about 8 large mangoes); peeled, pitted, and cut into rough chunks

$\frac{1}{3}$ cup fructose (or more to taste)

2 tablespoons fresh lime juice

Ingredients for Coconut Sorbet

1 tablespoon xantham gum

1 cup water

5 cups coconut milk

1 cup coconut flakes

¾ cup fructose (or more to taste)

1 pinch salt (optional)

1 tablespoon fresh lime juice

Ingredients for Lime Sorbet

1 tablespoon xantham gum

3 cups water

3 cups fresh lime juice

1 cup fructose (or more to taste)

Yields: 6 to 8 servings

Directions for all sorbet variations

In blender, combine 1 cup water with the xantham gum. The mixture will be thick and gummy. Transfer it to a small saucepan and heat until it starts to bubble rapidly.

Rinse any remaining raw xantham gum mixture out of blender, then transfer the heated mixture back into the clean blender. Add the remaining ingredients and blend until completely smooth.

Pour the mixture into an ice cream or sorbet maker and churn for about 15 minutes. Place in freezer and allow to freeze for at least 4 hours before serving.

Caribbean Pumpkin Mousse with Coconut Whipped Cream

When I first learned to make a light-and-fluffy vegan mousse, I wanted to expand my repertoire from predictable chocolate mousses to include more interesting flavors. Roasting calabaza in an oven on high-heat for about 40 minutes is the best way to make this recipe, but jarred or canned pumpkin works too. This is a great alternative to pumpkin pie on Thanksgiving.

Ingredients for Mousse

1 cup soy milk
1 cup fructose
1½ tablespoon agar
4 cups pumpkin purée
6 ounces silken tofu
1 teaspoon fresh ginger juice
1 tablespoon arrowroot powder or cornstarch
1 teaspoon cinnamon
½ teaspoon nutmeg
½ teaspoon allspice
½ teaspoon ground clove
¼ teaspoon salt

Ingredients for Coconut Whipped Cream

1¾ cups coconut milk
1½ tablespoons powdered fructose (grind
    fructose in a coffee mill)

Yields: 6 servings

See photo on page 163

In a large saucepan, combine the soy milk, fructose, and agar. Heat on medium heat for about 12 to 15 minutes or until the agar has dissolved. Transfer the hot liquid to a blender and blend with the rest of the mouse ingredients.

Return mixture to the large saucepan and heat on medium-high heat until it comes to a boil. Pour mousse into bowls or glasses and place in the refrigerator to cool for at least 1 hour before serving.

In the meantime, combine the ingredients for the coconut whipped cream in a mixing bowl until the powdered fructose has completely dissolved. Fill a whipped cream dispenser with the mixture. Keep the dispenser in the refrigerator.

When ready to serve, garnish each pumpkin mousse with coconut whipped cream and cinnamon.

Cuban Rum Cake with Mango Coulis

I learned a lot about baking from my grandmother. She had a collection of different recipes, all with simple, but interesting names: like 1-2-3 cake or one-bowl cake. The one that I loved the most was called "Whiskey Cake." Maybe it was idea of adding alcohol to a dessert that was so intriguing. Nonetheless, it turned me onto using alcohol in baking. My first use of it at the restaurant came in the form of this Cuban Rum Cake. Finish it up with some fresh mango coulis, and this dessert is a little slice of tropical heaven.

Ingredients for Cake

1½ cups flour
1½ tablespoons baking soda
¾ tablespoon baking powder
1½ cups fructose
6 ounces silken tofu
½ cup dark rum
½ cup canola oil
1½ tablespoons fresh lime juice
½ cup soy milk

Ingredients for Glaze

1 cup dark rum
2 tablespoons fructose

Ingredients for Mango Coulis

2 ripe mango; peeled, pitted and cut into
    rough chunks
2 to 3 tablespoons fructose (depending on
    sweetness of mangoes)
2 tablespoons water
1 tablespoon fresh lime juice

Yields: 8 servings

Preheat oven to 350º. Grease a 9-inch cake pan with ½ teaspoon canola oil. Set aside. Using a sifter, combine the cake's dry ingredients in a medium mixing bowl. Set aside.

In a blender, combine the cake's wet ingredients and process until no silken tofu chunks remain. Then, add the wet ingredients to the dry ingredients and mix with a whisk just until all ingredients are combined. The batter should be thick. Do not overmix or the end result will be tough and flat.

Pour the batter into the cake pan and bake for about 30 minutes. After the first 15 minutes, rotate the pan 180º to ensure even baking. The cake is done when it is golden brown and a toothpick inserted in its center comes out clean.

Remove the cake from the oven and allow it to cool on the counter for about 20 minutes. Then, run a kitchen knife around the sides of the cake to loosen it, and invert the cake onto a plate. If the cake does not pop out from the pan right away, cool it in the refrigerator for 10 minutes and then invert it again. Set aside.

Heat the rum and fructose in a saucepan until it flames and the alcohol begins to cook out. Allow the mixture to reduce by about half; it will be very thick and syrupy.

Pour the rum and fructose syrup over the top of the cake and then allow it to completely cool in the refrigerator for about 20 minutes.

Lastly, in a blender, combine the *Mango Coulis* ingredients until smooth. Chill in the refrigerator until ready to use. Then, slice the cake, drizzle each slice with the coulis and garnish with some fresh fruit or serve with soy ice cream.

Summertime Strawberry Shortcake

This is my tribute to a summertime favorite, complete with homemade whipped cream, or "chantilly" as the French would call it. As with any fresh whipped cream, it doesn't hold its shape for too long after using it, so I recommend decorating your shortcake right before serving. If you do not have a whipped cream dispenser, you could substitute the whipped cream with vanilla soy ice cream or a soy whipped cream. However, I highly recommend purchasing a whipped cream dispenser—they are fun to use and they provide very beautiful results.

Ingredients for Cake

1½ cups flour
2 teaspoons baking powder
1 teaspoon baking soda
1 stick soy margarine, softened
1 cup fructose
1 pinch salt
1 tablespoon vanilla extract
6 ounces silken tofu
1 cup soy milk
1½ tablespoons fresh lemon juice
3 tablespoons egg replacer
1½ tablespoons canola oil

Ingredients for Chantilly

1 cup coconut milk
½ cup soy creamer
1 tablespoon vanilla
½ teaspoon fresh lemon juice
1½ tablespoons powdered fructose (grind fructose in a coffee mill)

Ingredients for Strawberries

1 pint fresh strawberries
1 tablespoon fresh lemon juice
2 tablespoons fructose (optional)

Yields: 6 servings

See photo on page 159

Preheat oven to 350°. Grease a 9x11-inch sheet pan with ½ teaspoon canola oil. Set aide. Combine all the cake's dry ingredients in a medium mixing bowl. Set aside.

In a food processor, combine the soy margarine, fructose, salt, and vanilla extract and process until creamy. In a blender, add the silken tofu, soy milk, lemon juice, egg replacer, and canola oil and blend until no tofu chunks remain. Add contents of the blender to the food processor and combine until smooth.

Next, add contents of food processor to dry ingredients and stir using a whisk or spoon until all ingredients are well combined. The batter will be thick and fluffy. Do not overmix or the end result will be tough and flat.

Pour the batter into the greased sheet pan and place in the oven immediately. Bake for about 30 minutes. After the first 15 minutes, rotate the pan 180° to ensure even baking. The cake is done when it is golden brown and a toothpick inserted in its center comes out clean. Remove the cake from the oven, let it cool for about 20 minutes, and then place it in the refrigerator.

Combine the ingredients for the chantilly in a mixing bowl until the powdered fructose has completely dissolved. Fill a whipped cream dispenser with the chantilly ingredients and follow instructions for filling with a cartridge. Keep the dispenser in the refrigerator.

Lastly, hull and slice the strawberries about 15 minutes before serving. Toss them in a large bowl with the lemon juice and fructose. The citrus and sugar will make the tossed strawberries drop some of their liquid, and you get a beautiful red syrup as a result. Slice the cake in squares and stack layers of cake, chantilly, and strawberries. Garnish with fresh mint or whole strawberries.

Coconut Pastel de Tres Leches

Go to any Mexican restaurant and some version of tres leches or "three milk" cake will be on the dessert menu. Oddly enough, the tres leches is Nicaraguan in origin. A light sponge cake, it is traditionally soaked in a combination of condensed, sweetened-condensed, and whole milks. Then, it's topped with either icing or whipped cream. At the restaurant we serve a coconut-flavored version, which is much cleaner and better for you, but still as decadent as the original.

Ingredients for Cake

1½ cups flour
2 teaspoons baking powder
1 teaspoon baking soda
1 stick soy margarine
1 cup fructose
1 pinch salt
1 teaspoon vanilla extract
6 ounces silken tofu
1 cup coconut milk
1 tablespoon fresh lime juice
3 tablespoons egg replacer
1½ tablespoons canola oil

Ingredients for Three Milks

¼ cup rum
¼ cup soy milk or soy creamer
½ cup coconut milk
1½ tablespoons fructose
1½ tablespoons fresh lime juice

Ingredients for Coconut Whipped Cream

1¾ cups coconut milk
1½ tablespoons powdered fructose (grind fructose in a coffee mill)

Yields: 6 servings

See photo on page 163

Preheat oven to 350°. Grease a 9x11-inch sheet pan with ½ teaspoon canola oil. Set aside. Combine all dry ingredients in a medium mixing bowl. Set aside.

In a food processor, combine the soy margarine, fructose, salt, and vanilla extract and process until creamy. In a blender, combine the silken tofu, coconut milk, lime juice, egg replacer, and canola oil and process until no tofu chunks remain. Add the contents of blender to the food processor, and process until smooth. Then, add the contents of food processor to dry ingredients and stir using a whisk or spoon until all ingredients are well combined. The batter will be thick and fluffy. Do not overmix or the end result will be tough and flat.

Pour the batter into the greased sheet pan and place in the oven immediately. Bake for about 30 minutes. After the first 15 minutes, rotate the pan 180° to ensure even baking. The cake is done when it is golden brown and a toothpick inserted in its center comes out clean. Remove the cake from the oven, let it cool for about 20 minutes, and then place it in the refrigerator.

Combine the ingredients for the coconut whipped cream in a mixing bowl until the powdered fructose has completely dissolved. Fill a whipped cream dispenser with the mixture. Keep the dispenser in the refrigerator.

For the three milks, reduce the rum by heating it in a saucepan until it flames and all the alcohol cooks out. You will be left with about ⅛ cup. Combine the reduced rum and the other "three milks" ingredients in a medium mixing bowl.

When ready to serve, slice the cake in triangles and soak each slice in the "three milks." Stack two triangles of soaked cake with coconut whipped cream between and on top of them.

Mexican Chocolate Tower

Everyone loves a dessert with the word "tower" in the name, and one with chocolate and peanut butter is sure to please everyone. I use many traditional Mexican ingredients in this recipe as well as techniques, such as combining hot and cold components. The best part about this dessert is the impressive visual results.

Ingredients for Cake

1½ cups flour
2 teaspoons baking powder
1 teaspoon baking soda
1 tablespoon cocoa powder (optional)
1 stick soy margarine
½ cup fructose
1 cup semisweet chocolate chips (melted)
1 pinch salt
6 ounces silken tofu
1 cup soy milk
1½ tablespoons fresh lime juice
3 tablespoons egg replacer
1½ tablespoons canola oil

Ingredients for Peanut Butter Cream

1 cup peanut butter
½ cup sugar
½ teaspoon salt
½ cup soy milk or soy creamer
½ cup cold water

Ingredients for Mole Sauce

1 cup semisweet chocolate chips
¼ cup tequila
1¼ cup soy milk
1 tablespoon fresh lime juice
2 tablespoons toasted sesame seeds
⅛ cup walnuts (about 6 walnut halves, raw)
1 tablespoon cocoa powder
1 ancho chile, just flesh (no stems or seeds)
1 teaspoon cayenne (optional for extra heat!)
¼ cup fructose

Yields: 4 servings

See photo on page 164

Preheat oven to 350°. Grease a 12-cup muffin tin with 1 teaspoon canola oil. Set aside. In a medium mixing bowl, sift together dry cake ingredients. Set aside. Melt the chocolate chips in a saucepan on low heat, stirring constantly or in a microwave for about 1½ minutes. Combine the melted chocolate and the margarine, fructose, and salt in a food processor and process until smooth.

In a blender, combine the silken tofu, soy milk, lime juice, egg replacer, and oil, and blend until no tofu chunks remain. Add the contents of the blender to the food processor and mix until smooth. Add the wet ingredients to the dry ingredients and mix with a whisk just until all ingredients at combined. Do not overmix or the end result will be tough and flat.

Scoop the batter into the tins, about ½ cup per muffin, and place in the oven immediately. Bake for about 25 to 30 minutes or until a toothpick inserted into the center of any muffin comes out clean. After the first 15 minutes, rotate your muffin tins 180° to ensure even baking. Remove from the oven and allow muffins to cool for about 15 minutes before inverting onto a sheet pan. Allow them to cool fully for another 10 minutes.

Meanwhile, in a food processor, combine all the *Peanut Butter Cream* ingredients and process until smooth. Set aside. In a saucepan, heat all the *Mole Sauce* ingredients until they boil. Then, transfer them to a blender and purée until smooth. Be very careful when puréeing hot liquids! The heat and steam can cause the contents to burst out from beneath the lid. Always begin by pulsing the blender gradually, and then move to a steady purée.

To serve each dessert, layer three cakes with about 2 tablespoons of peanut butter cream between them and on top, using a pastry bag or spoon. Warm the mole sauce in a saucepan or the microwave and make a pool of it around each tower. Garnish with powdered cocoa.

Black Rainforest Cake

This is my version of the German classic Schwarzwaelder Kirschtorte, or Black Forest Cake. I sampled this rich dessert while visiting Munich. Traditionally, it is chocolate cake with sour cherries, whipped cream, and shaved chocolate. Incorporating the tropical inspiration ever present in Horizons cuisine, I've modified this recipe to celebrate the tropical rainforests around the world.

Ingredients for Cake

3 cups flour
3 tablespoons baking soda
1½ tablespoons baking powder
2 cups semisweet chocolate chips (melted)
3 cups fructose
12 ounces silken tofu
1 cup soy milk
½ cup dark rum
1 cup canola oil
3 tablespoons vinegar

Ingredients for Icing

6 tablespoons soy margarine, softened
6 tablespoons shortening, softened
2 cups powdered fructose (grind in coffee mill)
½ cup toasted macadamia nuts (allow to cool)
½ cup toasted cashews nuts (allow to cool)
2 teaspoons arrowroot powder or cornstarch
2 tablespoons vanilla extract
¼ cup cold water

Ingredients for Filling

1½ cups fresh lychees, halved and skinned
2 tablespoons fresh lime juice
2 tablespoons fructose

Guava Coulis

**1 cup guava pulp; peeled, seeded, and cut into
    rough chunks (fresh or frozen guava)**
2 teaspoons fresh lime juice
4 tablespoons fructose (or more to taste)
4 tablespoons water

Yields: 10 servings

See photo on page 162

Preheat oven to 350°. Grease two 9-inch cake pans with 1 tablespoon canola oil. Set aside. Using a sifter, combine the cake's dry ingredients in a large mixing bowl. Set aside. Melt the chocolate chips in a saucepan on low heat, stirring constantly (or melt them in a microwave for about 2 minutes). Then in a blender, combine all the other wet cake ingredients, and process until no tofu chunks remain.

Add the melted chocolate and blended wet ingredients to the dry ingredients and mix with a whisk just until all ingredients are combined. The batter should be thick. Do not overmix or the end result will be tough and flat.

Pour the batter into the cake pans and bake for about 30 minutes. After the first 15 minutes, rotate the pan 180° to ensure even baking. The cakes are done when a toothpick inserted into the center of each comes out clean.

Remove the pans from the oven and allow the cakes to cool on the counter for about 20 minutes. Then run a kitchen knife around the sides of each cake and invert each pan onto a plate. If the cakes do not pop out right away, cool them in the refrigerator for 10 minutes and invert them again. Chill the cakes in the refrigerator for another 30 minutes.

In a food processor, combine all the *Icing* ingredients until smooth. Set aside. In a blender, combine *Guava Coulis* ingredients until smooth. Set aside.

In a medium mixing bowl, combine the lychees with the lime juice and fructose. After a few minutes, the citrus and sugar will make the lychees drop some of their liquid and they will be soft and syrupy.

Finally, stack the layers of cake with ½ cup icing and ½ cup lychees between them. Top the cake with the remaining icing. Dust with shaved chocolate and garnish with tropical fruit.

Summertime Strawberry Shortcake (page 155)

Left: Banana Macadamia Nut Cinnamon Buns (page 146)
Top: Unfried Ice Cream with Cruzan Bananas (page 151)
Bottom: Winter Spiced Pear (page 150)

Black Rainforest Cake (page 158)

Top: Tart Tatin à l'Américain (pages 148-149)
Middle: Coconut Pastel de Tres Leches (page 156)
Bottom: Caribbean Pumpkin Mousse with Coconut Whipped Cream
(page 153)

Mexican Chocolate Tower (page 157)

Afterword

It's Saturday night in early May. The restaurant is packed, and there are people waiting at the door. In the excitement, I think to myself, "Wow! It's Saturday night, and all these people have come out for vegetarian food." Some 150 of them, by the time the night is done. I pause and reflect for a millisecond. I smile to myself contentedly. Never in my wildest dreams did I think it would have come this far. From the little lunch counter from which Horizons was born to this—a 10-year journey to this wonderful scene tonight!

Since Kate and I have been working together at Horizons, my restaurant life has changed in so many positive ways. For one, I have grown up and learned to work at the restaurant— not have the restaurant work me. The respect and passion Kate and I share at work breeds encouragement and inspiration. I can quite honestly say that I have never enjoyed my job as much as I do now.

So what about this place? What is Horizons? It doesn't even say "vegetarian restaurant" anywhere on its sign or menu! Well, the truth is that I don't like (and have never liked) to be labeled. I don't consider us a vegetarian restaurant. We are a restaurant like any other that just happens to not serve any animal meat.

That's the philosophy upon which Horizons was founded—the un-vegetarian vegetarian restaurant. I figured the vegetarians would find us and be happy. But it is the general public with whom I wanted to connect: people who would otherwise not be "caught dead" walking through the doors of a vegetarian café; the people who think we might serve them lentil loaf and steamed kale. Somehow it worked! And they are here. Especially tonight.

I pride us on the wonderfully diverse group that fills this place: auto mechanics, newscasters, lawyers, hippies, assorted baby-boomers, tattooed-and-pierced teens, singers, local small-business owners —a microcosm of America, all right here, eating tofu and seitan. A miracle indeed.

Well, that's enough reflecting. Back to work. Thank you all who asked for and bought this book. Thank you for all your encouragement through the years, especially those who have seen us grow through our three incarnations. This book is for all who support us and want a better life for yourself, your family, your community, and our civilization.

CHEF RICH
05 May 2003

That's a wrap!

. . . .

Index

Horizons: The Cookbook